CONTENTS

Gods Live in the Heavens 8

The First Astronomers 10

The Sun — The Giver of Life 12

The Sun's Family 14

Our Home Planet 16

Our Nearest Neighbour 18

The Milky Way and the Universe 20

Messengers from Space — Shooting Stars
and Comets 22

Nicolas Copernicus — The First Revolutionary 24

Johann Kepler — Astronomer and Astrologer 25

Galileo Galilei — The Creator of Modern
Science 26

Tycho Brahe — The Great Observer 27

Sir Isaac Newton — The Greatest Scientist 28

Time Through the Centuries 29

The Constellations — Legends in the Heavens 30

Sailing by the Stars 32

Telescopes Open Up the Universe 34

Probing the Depths of the Universe 36

Signals from Outer Space 38

The Greatest Mystery of All 40

Destinies in the Stars? 42

The Power of Reaction 44

Gravity — The Force that Brings Us Down
to Earth 46

The Most Unusual Job in the World 48

Highlights of the Space Age 50

Rockets — The Most Powerful Vehicles of All 52

Man on the Moon 54

Man-made Moons in the Heavens 56

The Air Around Us 58

Does Life Exist on Other Planets? 59

Moonbase 60

Index 62

Exploring the Universe

Václav Kvapil
Edited by Neil Ardley

Illustrated by
Theodor Rotrekl

Hamlyn
London • New York • Sydney • Toronto

Designed and produced by Artia for
The Hamlyn Publishing Group Limited
London • New York • Sydney • Toronto
Astronaut House, Feltham, Middlesex, England
© Copyright Artia 1976
Illustrations © Theodor Rotrekl 1976
© Copyright this edition The Hamlyn Publishing Group Limited 1976
ISBN 0 600 38160 9
Printed in Czechoslovakia by Svoboda
1/11/02/51

Cramped together in their tiny spacecraft, three astronauts are fired into space by a mighty rocket. They are leaving their home — the Earth — for a voyage into the unknown and will travel millions of kilometres before they return to our world. Their journey will be one of adventure, for a vast storehouse of new and exciting discoveries awaits them in space.

The astronauts' voyage symbolizes man's great quest into the unknown. From the earliest times; men have looked towards the heavens and wondered at what they could see there. Then they began to make observations of the heavens, using instruments such as the astrolabe shown below, which measures the positions of stars in the night sky. As their knowledge of the heavens increased, so did the Universe begin to unveil more and more of its secrets and mysteries. We have now leapt into space and stand poised before the Universe. Who cannot feel excited at what we shall find there?

Gods Live in the Heavens

Many thousands of years ago, man began to think about the world on which he found himself. He saw that the land always came to an end when he reached the ocean. He noticed that the ocean looked flat and so too did most of the land. Not surprisingly, he came to the conclusion that the whole world was flat. However, there was one important question that he could not answer quite so easily — where is the world?

Many ancient civilizations placed the world on the backs of animals. Some considered that a turtle carried the world on its shoulders, and others that three massive whales did so. The Indians placed the world on the backs of four strong elephants. The Babylonians could not think of an animal large enough to carry the world. They thought that the land was encircled by water and that it formed a huge plate that floated on the water. At the edges of the plate were mountains that supported the heavens.

There was more agreement when it came to an explanation of the heavens. Everyone noticed that the Sun rises at dawn, crosses the sky during the day and then sets at dusk. So too the Moon makes its stately way through the heavens at night. The Sun gives light and warmth and readily came to be worshipped, for without the Sun there can be no life on the Earth. The Moon also became a god or goddess, though usually of less importance than the sun god, and other divinities came to join the Sun and Moon in the sky. In many civilizations, the heavens therefore became the home of the gods before astronomers began to explain the true nature of the heavens.

Above: The ancient Egyptians worshipped the sun god Ra. During the day he rode across the sky on his boat from east to west. At night he passed through the dark caverns of the underworld, bringing light to the tormented souls there. Throughout the day, Ra took care to avoid the great serpent Apep, who sometimes succeeded in swallowing Ra and his boat. This was how eclipses of the Sun were explained.

Left: The ancient Egyptian god Atum. He is often identified with Ra. He wears the double crown of the pharaohs, and holds the sign of the Sun in his hand.

Above: The ancient Egyptians worshipped the Sun in many forms. Often, the god is represented in human form but he is also to be seen as a bird, or as a man with a bird's head. Sometimes the sun god takes the form of a man bearing the Sun's disc on his head. Around the disc is a sacred snake that spits fire and destroys the god's enemies. The sun god's sanctuary was at Heliopolis, which means sun town.

Below: A thousand years ago in Mexico there lived an Indian people known as the Aztecs. The Aztec Indians had many gods and the most feared was the sun god, Tezcatlipoca. As well as bringing the harvest, the sun god brought drought. He had to be pleased, so the Aztecs made human sacrifices at the summits of their huge pyramids in honour of the sun god.

Above: According to a Chinese fable, the body of a giant called Panku became the Earth, his eyes became the Sun and Moon, his blood the seas and his breath the wind.

Above right: A stone carving from ancient Babylon shows a king presenting his daughter to a goddess. In the sky hang three bodies — the planet Venus, the Moon and the Sun. These three heavenly bodies were worshipped under the names Ishtar, Sin and Shamash. The most important was the moon god Sin, and Shamash the sun god and Ishtar (Venus) the war goddess were his children. Sin was a symbol of good because he illuminated the darkness where evil-doers hid. Shamash was the god of justice. The goddess of war, Ishtar, was sometimes known as the goddess of love.

The First Astronomers

Although they had little idea of the true nature of the Earth and the heavens, the ancient Babylonians and Egyptians made good observations of the Sun, Moon, planets and stars. They wanted to know more about the heavens to please their gods and to help predict the changing seasons, so that crops would grow well. With such knowledge, the ancient Greek astronomer Thales in 585 BC successfully predicted the day when an eclipse of the Sun would happen. Other Greek astronomers made observations of the heavens and tried to work out what the Earth and the heavenly bodies are really like. Because they based their ideas on actual observations, their theories were likely to be correct. But their instruments were not very good, and often their results could be explained in more than one way. For example, Thales' pupil, Anaximander, suggest-

ed that the Earth is curved because the positions of the stars in the sky change if you travel from one place to another. But he thought the Earth was shaped like a cylinder. Later in the 500s BC, Pythagoras proposed correctly that the Earth is shaped like a ball. Only a few people believed him; most wondered how a person could stand on the underside of a ball without falling off.

However, other astronomers believed Pythagoras. Aristotle, who lived in the 300s BC, was one but he incorrectly believed that the Sun moves round the Earth. Aristarchus said, in about 260 BC, that the Earth moves round the Sun, but Aristotle was a very famous philosopher and he was believed instead. Eratosthenes later worked out the correct size of the Earth, but also was not believed because most people thought that his result was too large.

Left: An old map showing Ptolemy's ideas of the Universe. Ptolemy lived in Egypt in the AD 100s. He wrote a book called the *Almagest* that contained the theories of the ancient Greek astronomers, particularly those of Hipparchus who lived two centuries before. Hipparchus measured the correct distance of the Moon from the Earth and also drew the first star maps. But he followed Aristotle in believing that the Earth was the centre of the Universe. Aristotle thought that the Moon, planets and Sun moved in circles around the Earth and that the stars lay in a fixed sphere beyond. This theory is shown in Ptolemy's map. In the centre is the Earth and in order around it, shown by their astronomical symbols, move the Moon, Mercury, Venus, the Sun, Mars, Jupiter and Saturn.

Below: The motions of the planets in the sky did not exactly fit Aristotle's theory (because the Earth in fact moves round the Sun like the planets do). But Hipparchus suggested that as a planet moves in one large circle around the Earth, it also moves at the same time in another smaller circle called an epicycle. This theory almost explains the motions of the planets, and it was not disproved for many centuries.

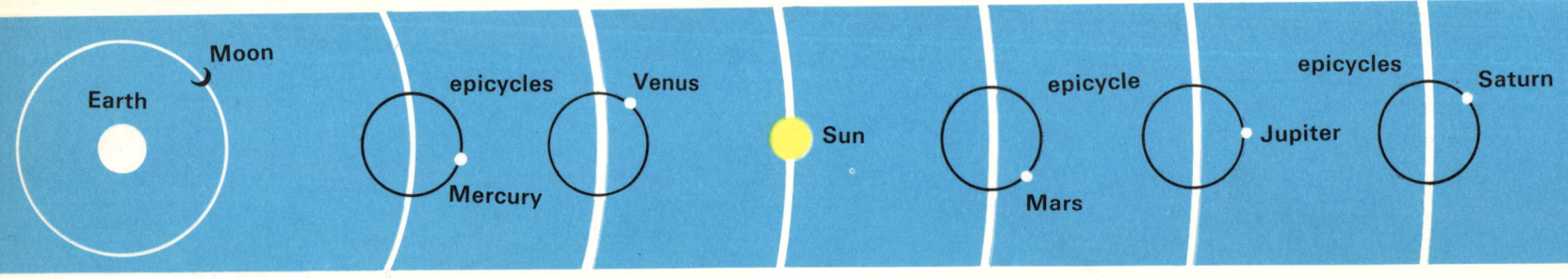

Above: An old map showing how the ancient Greeks pictured the world. It shows Europe, Africa and India and a suspected other continent. But the world is shown as a flat plate with all the land surrounded by the oceans.

Above: Ancient maps from other civilizations also show the world to be flat and surrounded by water. This picture, which dates from the 12th century and discovered in India, portrays this idea in a general way. The Chinese also had similar ideas about the world about this time.

Left: This map was engraved in clay in ancient times. It accurately shows the kingdom of King Sargon I of ancient Babylonia. It also depicts the known world entirely surrounded by water.

Right: Two Arab astronomers use astrolabes to measure the positions of the stars. The Arabs kept astronomy alive after Ptolemy's time, when little discovery took place in Europe.

Right: An engraving of the Middle Ages shows Aristotle holding a model which demonstrates his idea that the Sun moves around the Earth.

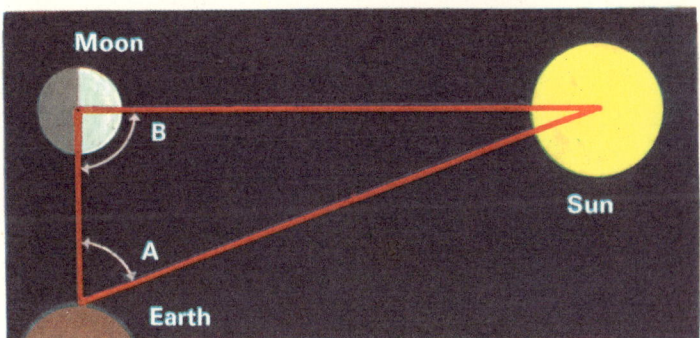

Above: The method by which the ancient Greek astronomer Aristarchus measured the comparative distance of the Moon and Sun from the Earth. When the Moon is half-full as shown, then the Moon, Sun and Earth must be at the corners of a right-angled triangle. That is, the angle **B** is a right angle. By measuring the angle **A**, which is the angle between the Sun and Moon in the sky, Aristarchus could find the comparative lengths of the sides of the triangle. He calculated that the Sun is 20 times as far from us as the Moon. His measurements were not accurate and in fact, it is about 400 times more distant.

The Sun — The Giver of Life

How far away is the Sun from us? Astronomers would say 149,504,200 kilometres. This is such a large figure that, to understand it, we must compare it with something we know. If we think of a train speeding along at 100 kilometres an hour, then it would have to travel for 170 years to cover the distance to the Sun. Even light, which travels at 300,000 kilometres a second, takes just over eight minutes to get to us from the Sun.

How big is the Sun? According to astronomers it has a diameter of 1,392,000 kilometres, which is 109 times the diameter of the Earth. In volume the Sun is more than a million times the size of the Earth. Once again, our train may give a better idea of the Sun's size — it would take 580 days or about a year and seven months to travel once round the Sun.

How hot is the Sun? It is so hot that a spaceship would melt and burn up long before it reached the Sun. The temperature at the surface is 6000 °C — far above the temperature at which even the most heat-resistant materials vaporize. And the temperature at its centre is about 14 million °C — a temperature so huge that nothing can compare with it.

How does the Sun shine? The Sun is in fact a star, and like all other stars is made up of very hot gases. All stars 'burn' their gases to produce light and heat in the same way. The gases do not burn like the gas in an oven or a gas fire, which needs the oxygen of the air to make a flame. In the Sun and stars, hydrogen gas is heated so much that it turns into helium, another gas. As it does so, it gives out more heat and the Sun or star keeps shining. The heat and light rays stream out through space in all directions. The Earth receives a very small share of these rays, but they are sufficient to keep us all alive. If the Sun were suddenly to go out, life would cease to exist on Earth. Fortunately, the Sun has enough hydrogen to keep shining for many more millions of years.

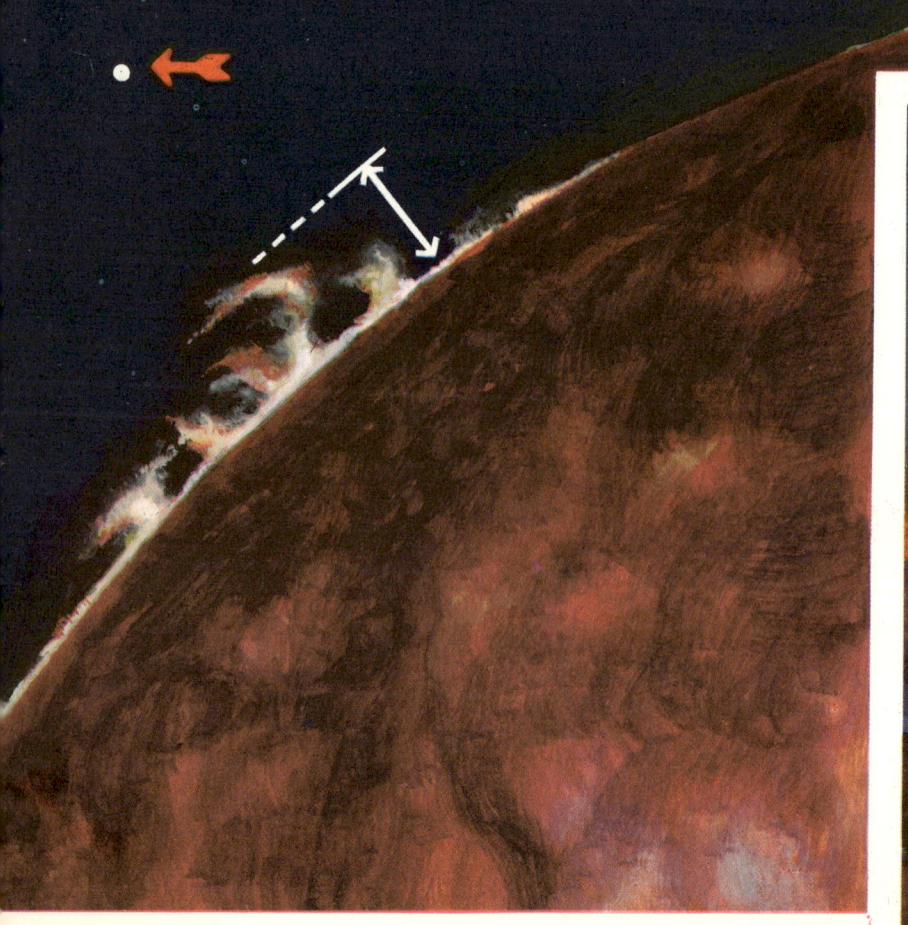

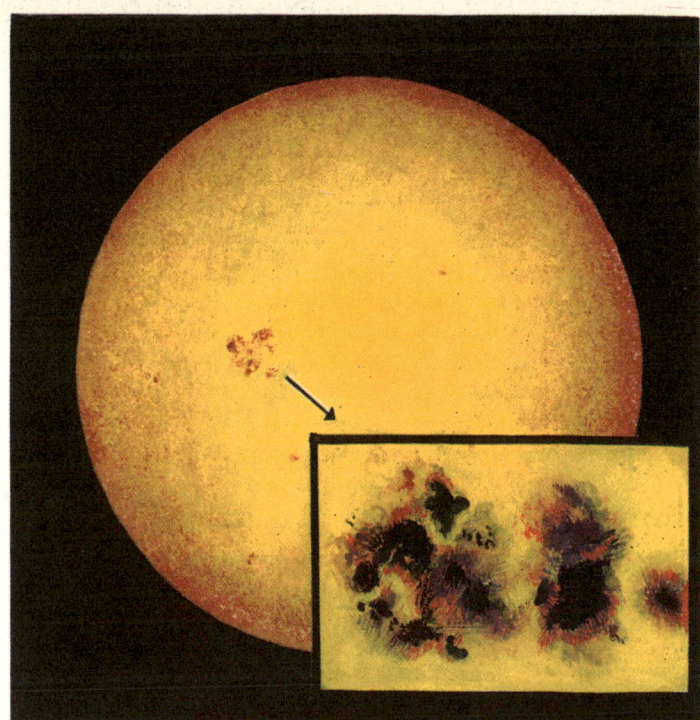

Right: The Sun has an atmosphere, but the Sun's surface is so bright that we cannot normally see it. However, during an eclipse of the Sun the surface is hidden by the Moon. The Sun's atmosphere then shows up around the Moon as a glowing cloud. The inner part of the Sun's atmosphere is called the chromosphere. Above it, the long rays of the solar corona reach out into space.

Above: The Sun looks like a glowing ball in the heavens. The surface is called the photosphere and it is made up millions of tiny grains of light. Often, great dark patches cross the Sun's surface. These are sunspots (inset), and they are like storms on the Sun. In fact, they are not dark but only less bright than their surroundings. Sunspots come and go, but greater numbers of them occur every 11 years. The next sunspot maximum will be in 1980. Sunspots are believed to affect the weather on Earth.

Below: A vast mass of glowing gas shoots up from the Sun's surface. These outbursts are called prominences and are seen when the Sun's surface is hidden during an eclipse.

Above: An eclipse of the Sun occurs when the Moon comes directly between the Sun and the Earth. The Moon's shadow just touches the Earth's surface, and anyone standing in the shadow sees the Sun's surface completely hidden by the Moon. This is a total eclipse. As the Moon moves, its shadow races over the Earth so that the eclipse is seen for a short time along a narrow path on the Earth's surface. Around this path is a broader zone, shown in blue, where only part of the Sun is hidden. Here, the Sun appears to have a piece bitten out of it, and this kind of eclipse is called a partial eclipse.

Opposite page: The Earth (red arrow) and the Sun to scale. The Earth has less than a hundredth of the Sun's diameter. The region above the Sun's surface denoted by the white arrow is the chromosphere. It is a layer of gas several thousand kilometres high. The great outbursts of glowing gas called prominences occur in the chromosphere. These can be seen only during an eclipse of the Sun, when the Sun's surface is hidden by the Moon. In ancient times people feared eclipses because they thought the Sun was disappearing for ever (inset).

Above: Many kinds of rays and particles reach us from the Sun. Particles (1) are deflected by the Earth's magnetic field into the radiation belts around the Earth. X-rays (2) and ultra-violet rays (3) are absorbed by the Earth's atmosphere. Light rays of all colours (4) reach us at the surface, as do infra-red rays (5) and radio waves (6). Particles from the radiation belts (7) may reach the Earth near the Poles, where they cause the bright lights in the sky known as the auroras.

The Sun's Family

The Earth is so close to the Sun that we see it as a glowing ball. All the other stars are so distant that they are just points of light in the sky. The Sun has a family of nine planets, of which the Earth is one. A planet is a solid body that moves around the Sun in a path that is almost a circle. Unlike the Sun, a planet does not glow and produce its own light. It is lit by the light from the Sun. Other bodies that are illuminated by the Sun can be seen in the heavens. They include the Moon, which moves around the Earth in the same way as the Earth moves around the Sun. Five of the other planets have their own moons circling around them. All these mem-bers of the Sun's family make up the Solar System. The family includes some more bodies, such as comets, asteroids and meteoroids. Other stars are believed to have their own families of planets and other bodies.

The Sun's planets, in order from the planet nearest the Sun to the most distant planet, are Mercury, Venus, Earth, Mars, Jupiter, Saturn, Uranus, Neptune and Pluto. Space probes containing automatic instruments have visited half of the other eight planets, but man himself has not yet reached beyond the Moon. Other planets may exist beyond Pluto, and some astronomers are searching for them.

Mercury

Venus

Mars

Jupiter

Saturn

Uranus

Neptune

Pluto

The planets of the Solar System fall into two groups. The first four planets are known as the inner planets. They are comparatively small planets. The largest is the Earth, and Venus is only a little smaller. Mars is about half the size of our planet, and Mercury is just under half the size of the Earth. Russian space probes have landed on Venus and Mars, but their instruments stopped working soon after landing and did not send back very much information about the surfaces of these planets. The Mariner space probes launched by the United States have flown near all the inner planets. From the pictures sent back, we know that both Mercury and Mars are covered with craters like the Moon. Mercury has almost no atmosphere and the gases in the atmosphere of Mars are not life-giving. Life as we know it could not therefore exist on these two planets. Venus is known as the mystery planet, because its surface is always hidden by clouds. We therefore have little idea of what the surface of Venus is like, but we do know that it is very hot there and that the atmosphere is unbreathable. Venus too must be a dead planet. Apart from Earth, the only inner planet to possess moons is Mars. It has two moons.

The first four of the five outer planets are known as the giant planets, for they are much larger than the inner planets. Jupiter is 11 times the size of the Earth, Saturn 9½ times, Uranus 3¾ times and Neptune 4 times. They also have many more moons. Jupiter has 12, Saturn 10, Uranus 5 and Neptune 2. Because they are so far from the Sun, the giant planets are far too cold for life. American Pioneer space probes have flown past Jupiter and sent back pictures of the Great Red Spot, a vast reddish area that is thought to be an immense storm raging on Jupiter. One probe is now flying on to Saturn and will reach the planet in 1979.

The farthest planet, Pluto, is very unlike the other outer planets. It has no moons and is about half the size of the Earth. Its orbit around the Sun sometimes brings it closer to us than Neptune. Many astronomers think that Pluto was once a moon of Neptune, but somehow escaped from its path around Neptune and became a planet instead.

Left: The planets of the Solar System, with their astronomical signs. The Earth is not shown.
Opposite page: The orbits of the planets (top) and the sizes of the Sun and planets to scale (bottom). The distances are not to scale.

15

Our Home Planet

The Earth has a very different face compared with the other bodies of the Solar System. The Moon, Mercury and Mars are dead worlds covered with craters, Venus is shrouded in whiteness, and the giant planets have only vague bands or markings. The Earth, on the other hand, is a beautiful planet. Great swirls of white cloud form an ever-changing pattern over the blue oceans and brown land. And it is very likely that our planet is the only one of the Sun's family to possess life.

How big is the Earth? At the Equator it is 40,009 kilometres around and 12,756 kilometres across. The Earth is slightly flattened at the Poles, its diameter from one Pole to the other being 43 kilometres less than at the Equator. Its mass is nearly 6 million million million million kilograms. The Earth takes 365¼ days to orbit once around the Sun, and this is the true length of a year. But we have three years of 365 whole days and then one leap year of 366 days to make up the extra quarter of a day. The Earth is shown below as it appears to astronauts travelling to the Moon.

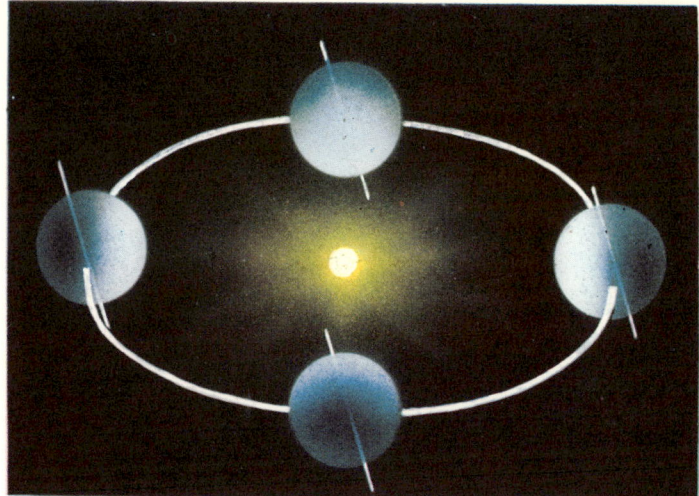

Above: The Earth's axis is tilted at an angle to its path around the Sun. The angle is 23½°. The direction of the tilt remains the same as the Earth orbits the Sun, so that first one pole is tilted towards the Sun and then the other. The existence of this tilt gives us the seasons. When the North Pole is tilted towards the Sun (right), it is summer in the northern hemisphere and winter in the southern hemisphere. When the South Pole tilts towards the Sun (left), it is summer in the southern hemisphere and winter in the northern hemisphere.

Left: The Earth's axis is an imaginary line joining the North and South Poles (top left). As the Earth spins on this axis, the axis itself wobbles very slowly. This wobble is called precession. It takes 26,000 years for the axis to make one complete circle. Its motion in this period is shown in the diagram top right. The other two diagrams show another movement of the Earth — the movement of the Earth-Moon system. These two bodies revolve about their centre of gravity, which is a point inside the Earth's surface. A point on the surface of the Earth moves around the centre of gravity and therefore follows a curved path through space.

Below: Stonehenge is an ancient monument in England. It is situated near Amesbury in Wiltshire, and it consisted of circles of huge stone arches. The earliest remains at Stonehenge date from about 2000 BC. Stonehenge is believed to have been some kind of temple used to worship the Sun. Some archeologists believe that it might have been used to predict when eclipses would occur. This could have been done from the positions of the shadows of the stone arches, but the mathematics needed to make such calculations are difficult.

Right: The position of the Sun in the sky varies from one season to another. In summer (top), it is high; in spring and autumn, it is at a medium height; and in winter, it is low in the sky. The lengths of shadows and the temperature vary accordingly.

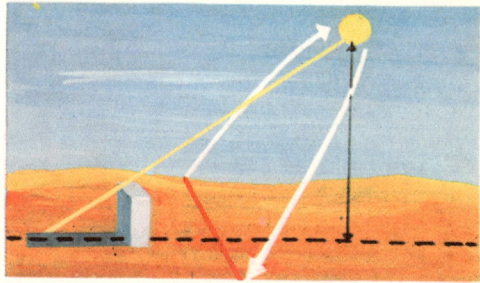

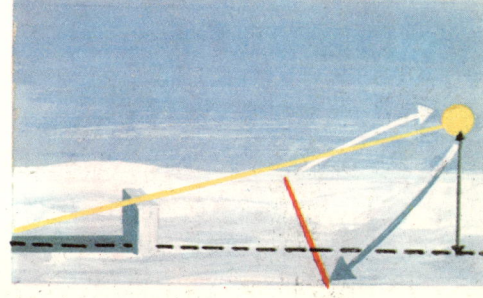

Our Nearest Neighbour

The nearest heavenly body to the Earth is the Moon. It is an average distance of 384,000 kilometres from us, which is just over 30 times the diameter of the Earth. The Moon's diameter is 3,476 kilometres, which makes it the same width as Australia. It orbits the Earth once every 27⅓ days and it also spins once in this time. This means that the Moon always points the same face towards the Earth, and we can never see the other side. Space probes have photographed the hidden side, which has more craters than the side we can see.

The Apollo astronauts brought back rocks from the Moon that showed it to be composed of similar rocks to those on Earth. However, being on the Moon is not like being on Earth. There is no air, which is why the sky appears black and the astronauts must wear spacesuits. The force of gravity is less, so that everything weighs only one-sixth of its weight on Earth. It is boiling hot in the sunlight, and far colder than freezing at night. The moonlight that we see on Earth is sunlight reflected by the Moon's surface.

The Moon probably formed separately from the Earth and then moved into orbit around our planet.

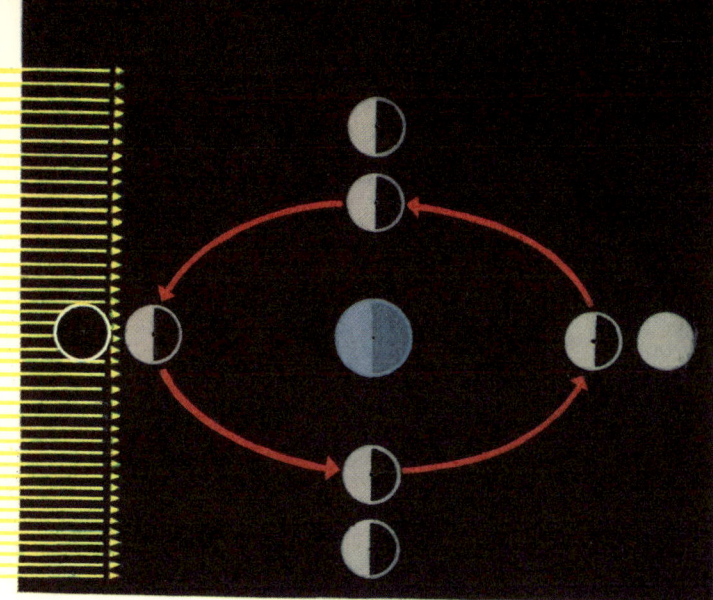

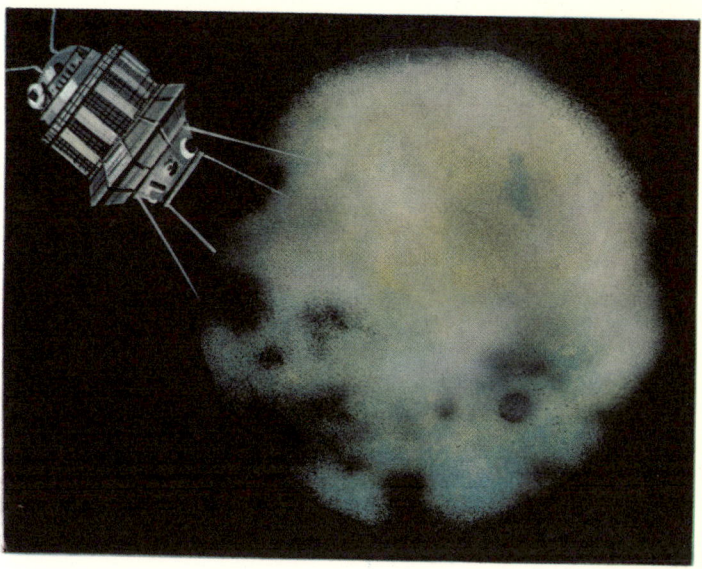

Above: The phases of the Moon are produced as the Moon moves around the Earth. At new moon (left), the Moon is dark because the side lit by the Sun is hidden from us. Then as the Moon moves to one side we see a small part of the illuminated side. It looks like a C backwards. This crescent grows until, at first quarter, we see a half-moon shaped like a D (bottom). This grows to a full moon when all of the illuminated side of the Moon is towards us (right). Then the full moon lessens to a half moon shaped like a D backwards at last quarter (top), and the half moon shrinks to a C-shaped crescent before it is new moon again. The whole cycle of these phases takes 29½ days.

Above: Modern Moon exploration began with the flight of the Russian space probe Luna 3 in 1959. This probe sent us our first view of the Moon's far side, which is always hidden from the Earth. Its shadowy picture showed several features of this unknown world.

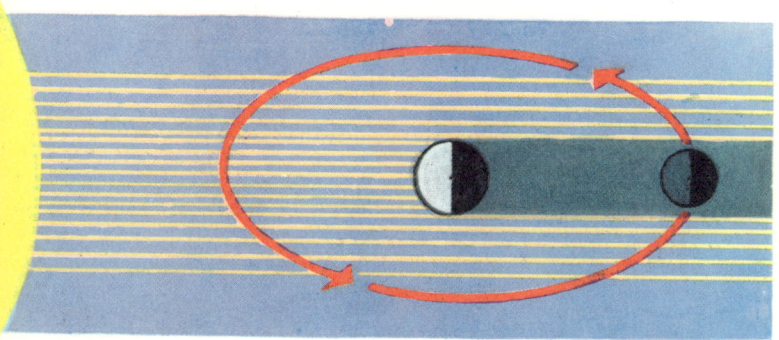

Above: An eclipse of the Moon occurs when the Earth comes directly between the Sun and the Moon. As it moves around the Earth, the Moon passes into the Earth's shadow and is hidden from view for a short time. It was the round shape of the Earth's shadow on the Moon during an eclipse that first told astronomers that the Earth is round. There are usually two eclipses of the Moon every year. Because an eclipse can be viewed from large areas of the Earth's surface, eclipses of the Moon are seen by many more people than eclipses of the Sun.

Opposite page: The Moon is covered with a vast number of craters, some of which are 100 kilometres or more in diameter. There are also high mountain ranges and vast plains. The craters are named after famous people, usually astronomers, and the plains are called seas. The first Moon landing was on the Sea of Tranquillity, which is to the right of the Moon as we see it from Earth. If you were suddenly transported to the Moon, you would be able to lift very heavy objects with ease, because everything on the Moon has only a sixth of the weight it would have on Earth (left). The Moon's symbol is a crescent shaped like the new moon (right).

Right: The photograph and map are of the crater Copernicus, a huge crater near the centre of the near side of the Moon. From 1966 to 1968, American Lunar Orbiter probes photographed the entire surface of the Moon in great detail, and excellent maps have been made from these pictures.

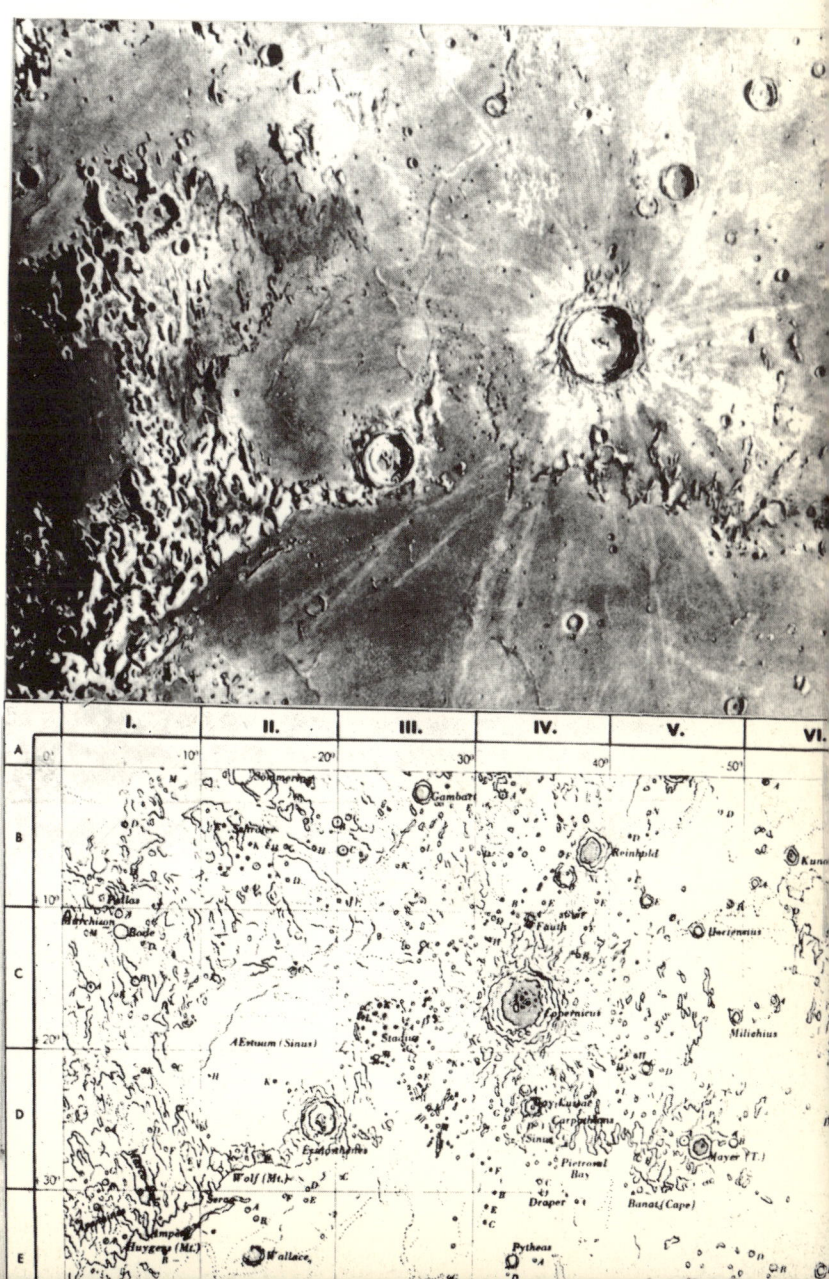

The Milky Way and the Universe

The Sun is not the only star in the sky, as you can easily see on a clear night. If you tried to count the stars in the night sky, you would make out several hundred. But the true number of stars in the sky is almost beyond belief, for millions upon millions more can be seen with the largest telescopes.

In fact, the Sun is just one of 100,000 million stars in a great wheel-shaped group of stars called the Galaxy. If you look at the Milky Way, the great band of stars that crosses the sky, you are looking into the Galaxy and its multitude of stars. The stars are arranged in long spiral arms around a central cluster of stars. The Sun lies towards the edge.

The Galaxy is immense. It is so large that it takes light 100,000 years to cross the Galaxy. Compare this with the time it takes light to reach us from the Moon — 1¼ seconds! Astronomers use light-years to measure the vast distances of the Universe. One light-year — the distance that light travels in a year — is equal to 9.5 million million kilometres. The Galaxy is rotating and it takes the Sun 225 million years to complete one revolution about the centre. As the Galaxy itself also moves through space, the Sun makes a slow spiral path through the Universe.

Just as our Sun is one of millions in the Galaxy, so too our Galaxy is just one of millions of other great groups of stars. These groups are also known as galaxies. They are to be found throughout space as far away as our telescopes can reach. Our telescopes can detect galaxies several thousands of millions of light-years away from us.

All the galaxies in the Universe are moving away from each other. This means that the Universe is getting bigger. Whether it will continue to get bigger or one day stop expanding no-one knows.

Many astronomers believe that the Universe began about 10,000 million years ago. All the matter in the Universe was gathered in a small space and it exploded in a 'big bang'. The stars formed as this matter rushed out into space.

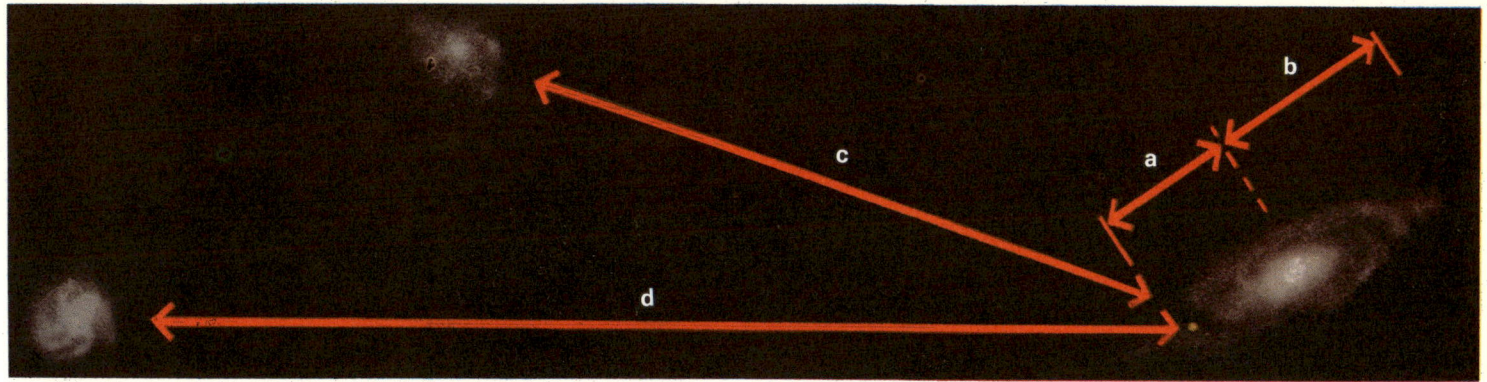

Above: The kilometre is not a very useful measurement for the vast distances that astronomers have to measure. It is as if we were to measure the size of the Earth in millimetres! So astronomers use the light-year, which is the distance light travels in one year. One light-year is equal to 9.5 million million kilometres. Even so, the figures are large. The Sun is 30,000 light-years from the centre of our Galaxy (a), and the Galaxy has a radius (b) of 50,000 light-years. The galaxy in Andromeda (c) is over 2 million light-years away, and the most distant galaxies (d) that we can see with a telescope are 5,000 million light-years distant from the Earth!

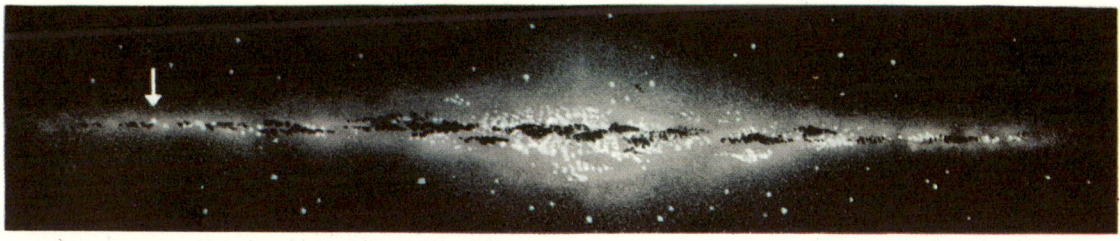

Above: Our Galaxy is a wheel-shaped group of 100,000 million stars. There is a dense cluster of stars at the central hub of the Galaxy and the other stars are strung out in long spiral arms around the centre. The position of the Sun is indicated by an arrow. The Galaxy is 100,000 light-years across, 20,000 light-years thick at the centre and only 3,000 light-years thick at the spiral arms. It is classed as a spiral galaxy because of its shape.

Right: Sir William Herschel was a German musician who came to England in 1757 and took up astronomy. He built the best telescopes then in existence and with them discovered the planet Uranus in 1781.

Above: The nearest galaxy to our own is the galaxy in the constellation of Andromeda, apart from the two Magellanic Clouds, which are satellite galaxies to our Galaxy. The Magellanic Clouds can be seen only in the southern hemisphere. The Andromeda galaxy is made up of many millions of stars arranged in spiral arms around a central cluster, as in our own Galaxy. It lies over 2 million light-years away, and is twice the size of our Galaxy.

Above: Many light or dark patches are to be seen when we look at our Galaxy. These patches are called nebulae, and they consist of misty clouds of gases and dust in space. The light nebulae either produce their own light and shine by reflecting light from the stars within them. Dark nebulae obscure light coming from the stars and stand out against a light background. The dark nebula shown above is called the Horse's Head.

Messengers from Space — Shooting Stars and Comets

If you keep a watch on the night sky, you will probably see several shooting stars during a single evening. They hurl themselves rapidly across the heavens in a trail of light. Shooting stars are fast-moving grains of metal or stone that burn up as they strike the Earth's atmosphere. Astronomers call shooting stars meteors. Sometimes, a meteor is large enough to survive its fiery flight through the air and strikes the ground. It breaks up in an explosion and carves out a crater in the ground. These bodies are called meteorites and they bring us messages from space. The message they bring is that life does probably exist somewhere else in space, because the meteorites contain chemical compounds that are to be found only in living things. However, as we do not

know where meteorites come from, we cannot be sure where life does exist elsewhere in the Universe. Comets move through the Solar System in paths rather like those of planets. They pass near the Sun and then move out into the far depths of space, not to return for many years or never to return. Sometimes a comet passes near the Earth. It does not speed across the sky like a shooting star. It moves very slowly across the sky over several days or even weeks. A comet consists of a small head and a long tail, both made up of clouds of dust. It can be seen because it is lit by light from the Sun.

Comets bright enough to be seen without a telescope are not frequent, but you are likely to see at least one in your lifetime.

Left: Halley's comet was discovered by the English astronomer Edmund Halley. In 1682, Halley saw the comet and thought that it might be the same comet as one seen early that century and in previous centuries. He predicted that it would return every 76 years. Halley was correct, although he did not live to see its next appearance. Halley's comet was last seen in 1910 and is expected again in 1986. When it is away from the centre of the Solar System, it recedes to far beyond Saturn. Halley's comet is a spectacular sight and it is the best comet that people are likely to see in their lifetime.

Below left: Crude drawings of comets have been found that date from ancient times.

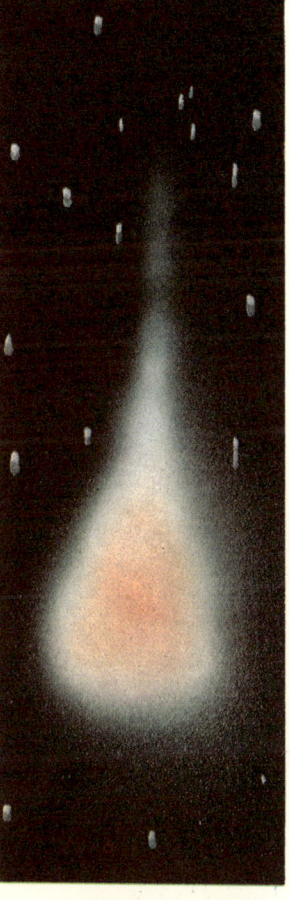

Above right: A photograph of a comet taken through a telescope often has streaks behind it. These are stars, and they appear as streaks because the telescope moved to follow the comet as the photograph was taken.

Opposite page: A group of terrified herdsmen witness the appearance of a meteorite. Many years ago meteorites caused fear in people.

Above: The largest meteorite ever found. It was discovered in Namibia (Southwest Africa) in 1920 and it weighs 59,000 kilograms. A large meteorite seldom falls to Earth; when it does it often breaks up on impact or before it hits the ground. There are two main classes of meteorites: metallic meteorites made of iron and nickel alloys and stony meteorites composed of minerals.

Above: The crater formed by the impact of a huge meteorite in prehistoric times. It is situated in Arizona in the United States and it is 1,280 metres across and 174 metres deep. Some fragments of the meteorite have been found in the crater, but the original meteorite must have weighed many thousands of tons. If a meteorite of such size hit a city, it would destroy it. Happily, such an event is almost certain never to occur.

Above: On 30 June 1908 a mysterious explosion shook the forest in the remote Tunguska region of Siberia. A force as great as that produced by the most powerful nuclear weapon devasted an area about 60 kilometres across. It was felt a thousand kilometres away. Many people supposed that a vast meteorite had hit the ground, but no crater was ever found. It is possible that a small comet may have hit the ground, but the mystery has never been satisfactorily explained.

Nicolas Copernicus — The First Revolutionary

Canon Copernicus served at the cathedral at Frauenburg in Poland. He was also a doctor and lawyer, but his great interest was astronomy. Copernicus lived from 1473 to 1543, and at this time people still believed that the Earth was the centre of the Universe and that the Sun moved around the Earth. But Copernicus realized that the Earth and other planets move around the Sun.

Copernicus' views had been put forward by others, notably the Greek astronomer Aristarchus. But Copernicus worked out his ideas mathematically. Nevertheless, the Church insisted that the Earth was the centre of the Universe and Copernicus did not publish his book, *The Revolutions of the Heavenly Orbs,* until he lay on his death bed. It caused a revolution in astronomy. Indeed, this use of the word revolution comes from the way in which Copernicus held that the Earth moves around the Sun.

Johann Kepler — Astronomer and Astrologer

Johann Kepler was born at Württemberg in Germany two years before Copernicus died. The timbered house where he was born is shown below. Kepler was a brilliant astronomer, and he was also interested in astrology — trying to predict the future by the movements of the planets and stars in the heavens. Kepler lived at a time when religious disputes caused much unrest. In 1600 he went to Prague in Bohemia (now Czechoslovakia) to work with astronomer Tycho Brahe, and he became the imperial mathematician to the Holy Roman Emperor. Tycho was a superb observer of the heavens, and Kepler was an excellent mathematician. In Prague Kepler was able to follow Copernicus in believing the Earth and planets moved around the Sun, but he soon realized from Tycho's observations that they did not move in circles as Copernicus thought. He tried to find out which kind of curve fitted the motions of the planets and eventually worked out that they must move in ellipses instead of circles. An ellipse has an oval shape. Kepler also made two other discoveries about the movements of the planets, and the three findings are known as Kepler's laws of planetary motion. They remain true today, over three centuries later.

Kepler also developed the science of optics. The astronomical telescope is called the Kepler telescope after him. Kepler died in Germany in 1630.

Galileo Galilei — The Creator of Modern Science

Below you can see a large room in a palace and two people arguing. The well-dressed bearded man without a hat is Galileo, who lived in Italy from 1564 to 1642. He was the greatest scientist of his time, and is now known as the father of modern science because he invented the kinds of methods by which scientists nowadays prove things are true. The man dressed in red robes is important because he is a cardinal of the Catholic church.

The year is 1633 and Galileo is on trial. He is a follower of Copernicus and has written books declaring that the Earth moves round the Sun. The church believes that the Earth is the centre of the Universe and that the Sun moves round the Earth. In Italy at this time no-one is allowed to disagree with the church. In great fear lest he should be burned at the stake, Galileo takes back his views and says that the church is right after all.

Galileo was the first astronomer to use the telescope. With it he made many discoveries. Among these was the discovery that Venus has phases like those of the Moon. This could only be true if Venus circled the Sun, and Galileo believed that this finally showed that the Earth too circled the Sun. Most people agreed, and the views of the church did not last long after Galileo's trial.

Tycho Brahe — The Great Observer

In 1560 there was an eclipse of the Sun. It so impressed a young Dane called Tycho Brahe that he decided to take up astronomy. He began to observe the skies with unaided eyes, for this was before the invention of the telescope. In 1572 Tycho observed that a bright new star suddenly appeared in the heavens. The star was a nova, or an exploding star, and Tycho's discovery made his name as an astronomer. The King of Denmark built him the best observatory in the world, on the island of Hven.

Tycho found that the tables of stars then in existence were not accurate and he made thousands of observations to improve our knowledge of the positions of stars in the sky. In 1597 he went to work in Prague in Czechoslovakia. He died only four years later. Tycho's assistant, Johann Kepler, took his observations and used them to discover the true motions of the planets.

Tycho was the last great astronomer to observe the heavens without a telescope. He was also the last great astronomer to hold that the Sun moved around the Earth. However, to explain the movements of the planets, he believed that the Sun moved round the Earth and, as it did so, all the other planets moved round the Sun! Few people could agree with such a complicated theory.

Tycho Brahe's accurate observations of the stars, made without a telescope, enabled Johann Kepler to find the true paths of the planets through the heavens.

Tycho's brass celestial sphere, nearly two metres in diameter, has about a thousand stars marked on it, probably by Tycho himself.

Sir Isaac Newton — The Greatest Scientist

Many people consider Sir Isaac Newton, who lived in England from 1642 to 1727, to be the greatest scientist who has ever lived. He discovered new kinds of mathematics, demonstrated the true nature of light and invented the reflecting telescope that astronomers use, and worked out the laws by which everything moves. He also asked himself *why* the planets and moons move as they do.

Newton said that this idea came to him when he saw an apple fall from a tree. He wondered if the force which must pull the apple to the ground stops the Moon from flying out into space and keeps it moving round the Earth. He reasoned that every object has a force of gravity that pulls other objects towards it. The force is greater if the object is bigger, which is why things weigh more on the Earth than on the Moon. Also, the force is smaller if the objects are farther apart.

The Moon circles the Earth and the planets move around the Sun because, as they move through space, the gravity between them pulls the smaller bodies into orbits around the larger body. There is no air in space to slow the bodies down, and so they keep moving in their orbits.

Above: Newton placed a glass prism in the path of a ray of sunlight that entered his darkened room through a chink in the door or the curtains. He noticed that several stripes of coloured light emerged from the prism. This band of colours is called a spectrum and you can observe it in a rainbow, because the rain drops act as tiny prisms. Newton's experiment showed that white light is in fact made up of several colours combined together. This principle is used in colour photography and colour television today.

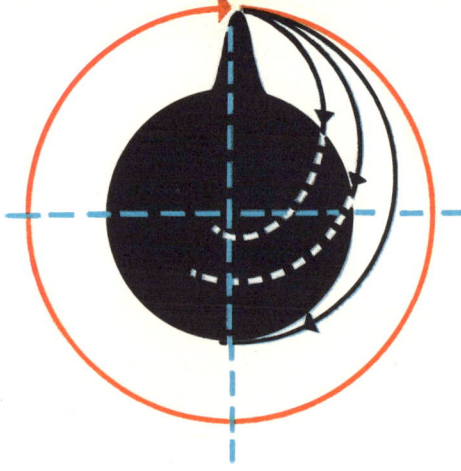

Above: Ideas of the true nature of the Universe were confused in earlier times, as the top picture shows. Newton showed how the force of gravity holds the planets and moons in their orbits. The bottom diagram shows what happens if you throw a stone out from a high hill. Gravity pulls it down, bending its path into a curve. The harder you throw, the farther it travels before it hits the ground. If you could throw it fast enough, gravity would pull it into a curving orbit right around the world (red line). If nothing stopped it, the stone would orbit the Earth for ever.

Time Through the Centuries

Man has not always looked to the skies just in curiosity. Basically, we measure time by the movement of the Earth — for example, one hour is a 24th part of the time it takes the Earth to spin once on its axis. A year is the time it takes the Earth to go once round the Sun. These quantities of time can be measured exactly only by observing the positions of the stars.

We now know from precise observations that one year lasts exactly 365 days 5 hours 48 minutes and 46 seconds. But earlier people did not know the exact length. The ancient Egyptians had years of 365 days each, so that their calendar slowly got out of order with the seasons. The Romans therefore introduced a calendar in which every fourth year (every year that can be divided by four) is a leap year of 366 days, making the average length of a year 365¼ days. This is 11 minutes 14 seconds too long. By the 1500s, this calendar was ten days out. So the ten days were lost and the calendar changed so that every century year, such as 1800 and 1900, is not a leap year except when the date can be divided by 400, as in 2000. In this calendar, the year is the correct length to within a few seconds.

1. A Roman sundial — the position of the shadow marks the hour.
2. An oil clock — the level of the oil shows the time.
3. The astronomical clock at the cathedral in Strasbourg, France. It shows many different times.
4. A Roman calendar. The days are marked on the outside and months (shown by signs of the zodiac) in the centre.
5. A water-clock of ingenious construction — as the water level changes, the pointer moves round the dial.
6. A German sundial made in 1700.
7. A weight-driven clock.
8. A modern quartz clock. It contains a quartz crystal that vibrates at a precise rate to regulate the clock, which is extremely accurate.

The Constellations — Legends in the Heavens

If you live in the northern hemisphere, you may be able to look at the stars in the sky and make out the outlines of the human figures and animals shown in the old star map illustrated below. The stars make up groups called constellations and each constellation has the name of a legendary animal or person. Here you can see the Great Bear near the centre and, to the right, the Lion apparently trying to eat the Crab (which here looks more like a lobster). On the other side of the centre, the Swan is flying near Pegasus, the winged horse of legend. You will also see that the constellations have Latin names — Leo for Lion and Cancer for Crab, for example. Astronomers prefer to use Latin names rather than trans-

late names into many different languages.

Ancient peoples gave the constellations their names and we still use them today because they are as good as any other names we could think of. The brighter stars have old names too; names like Sirius, Aldebaran, Mira and Algol. Many of these names are Arabic. However, most of the stars in the sky do not have special names. They are named with a Greek letter and a constellation name, such as Alpha Centauri. This means that it is the first star in the constellation Centaurus. Many faint stars that can be seen only in telescopes are simply given letters and numbers that denote their position in a particular star catalogue.

Above: An Arabic illustration of Ophiuchus, the serpent bearer.

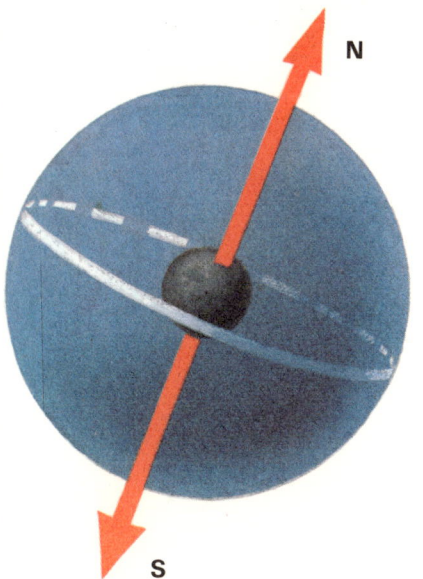

Above: A map of the constellations around the Pole Star in the northern skies.

Left: The North Pole lies directly beneath the Pole Star. As the Earth rotates, so the northern constellations appear to move in circles around the Pole Star. There is no star directly above the South Pole, and the southern constellations circle around the point above the Pole.

Below: A map of the constellations around the Southern Cross in the southern hemisphere.

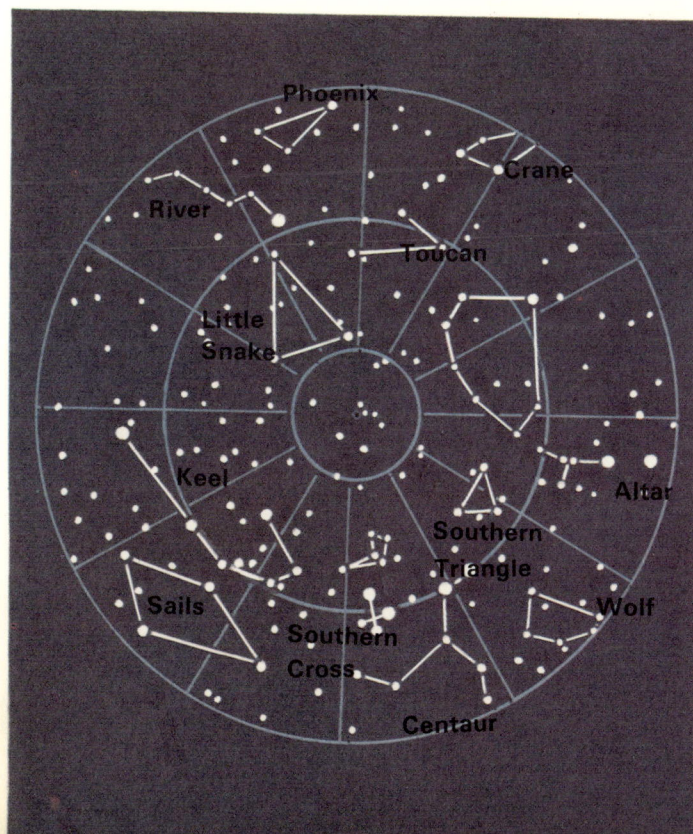

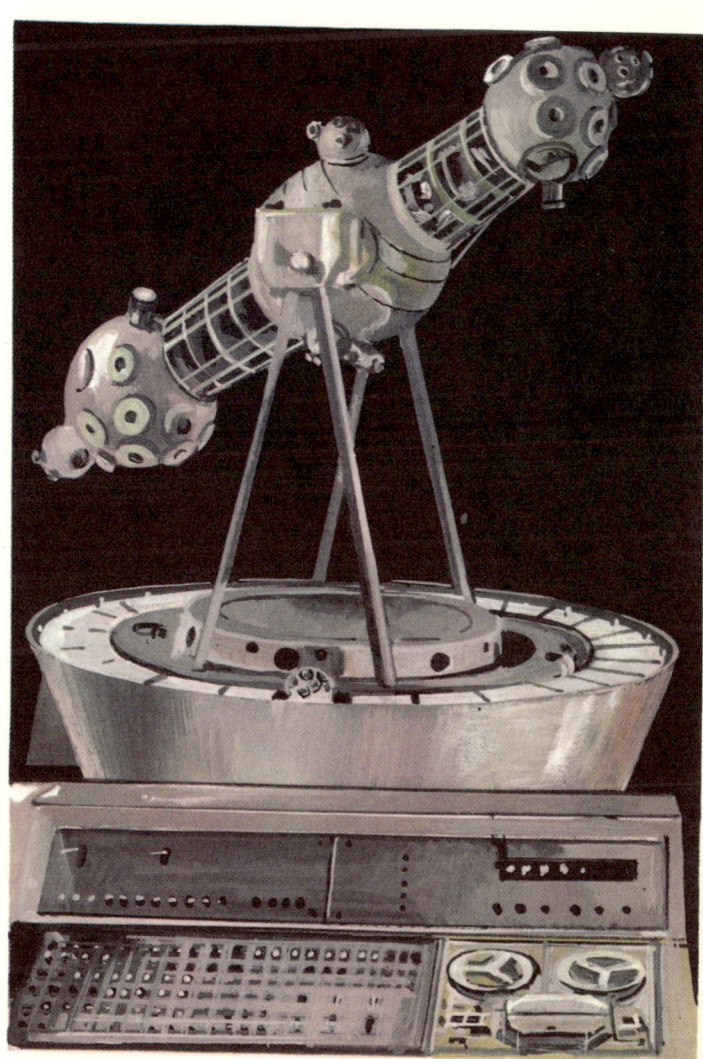

Above: This strange insect-like machine is the projector of a planetarium. Before it is the control panel of the planetarium. A planetarium is a building in which an accurate picture of starry heavens is shown on a dome-shaped ceiling. The projector contains many lenses, which all move in various ways so that the stars appear to move over the dome just as they move through the night sky. People who live in cities cannot see the stars easily because of the street lights along the roads. Visiting a planetarium is a startling experience, for there the heavens appear in all their glory.

Sailing by the Stars

Most of the early civilizations grew up on the shores of the Mediterranean Sea. This is not a large sea and it was not difficult for mariners to find their way from one port to another. But when they set sail on the great oceans, finding their way became more difficult. Usually, they tried to follow the coastline but eventually they began to navigate the open sea. How did these intrepid mariners find their way? The position of the Sun in the sky gave some idea of their direction, but it was no help when the weather was cloudy. In about AD 1200, sailors began to use the magnetic compass to find their direction.

They could estimate their speed by trailing a log in the water and find the distance travelled every day. In this way, they made a rough guess of their position.

Navigation became easier with the introduction of latitude and longitude. By simply measuring the angle of the Pole Star above the horizon, the ship's latitude is found. The longitude can be found by knowing the exact time at which the Sun or a particular star reaches a certain position in the heavens. Good navigation was therefore not possible before accurate clocks were invented in the 1700s.

Above: The magnetic compass came into use in Europe in about AD 1200, but it is possible that it originated in China centuries before. The Chinese had a kind of magnetic spoon; when spun, it would most often have come to rest pointing north-south, like a compass needle. The first compasses were much simpler and consisted of a dish of water in which floated a small piece of wood to which a magnetized iron needle was attached. The needle always turned to point to the magnetic North Pole, which is near the true North Pole.

Below: Sailors estimated their speed by using a log. This was a piece of wood attached to a knotted rope. The log was thrown overboard and trailed behind the boat. The rope was paid out so that the log remained still in the water, and the number of knots passing through the sailor's hands were counted. From this, the speed could be found. Ship's speeds are still measured in knots.

Above: A much easier way of finding the speed of a vessel is to use a taffrail log. This consists of a rotator with spiral fins that spins as it is pulled through the water. The line towing the rotator also spins and is connected to a registering device with a dial like a clock. The dial shows the distance travelled from a particular point. By measuring the distance travelled in a certain time, the ship's speed can be calculated.

Left: The magnetic compass has now been replaced by the gyro-compass. At the heart of this instrument is a spinning gyroscope mounted so that it can turn in any direction. The gyroscope always remains pointing in the direction in which it is first set, no matter how the ship moves. The gyroscope is therefore set to face north and a compass card is attached to it so that the ship's direction can easily be read.

Opposite page: The early mariners had only an hourglass to help them in finding the longitude of a ship's position. Finding the latitude was easier. The navigator used a device called a quadrant to measure the angle of the Pole Star above the horizon. He held the lower arm horizontal and moved the upper arm until he was looking directly along it at the Pole Star. The angle between the upper and lower arms gave the required angle, which is the same as the latitude.

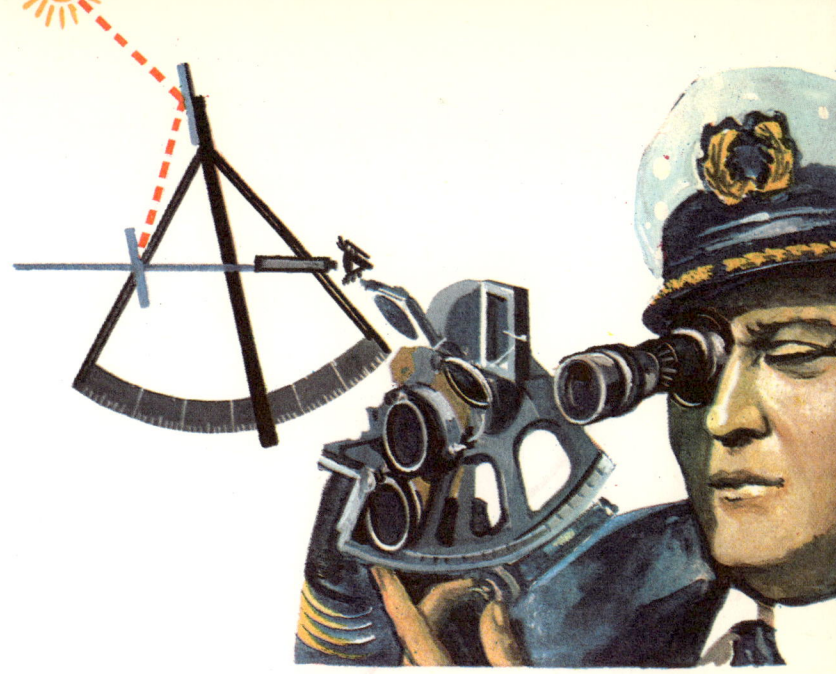

Above: In the 1700s, navigation became much simpler with the invention of chronometers (accurate clocks) to keep time and the sextant, which easily measures the angles that the Sun and stars make with the horizon. The navigator simply peers through the telescope on the instrument into a piece of glass called the horizon glass. This is half glass and half mirror. He looks through the glass half at the horizon and in the mirror half he sees a reflection of the sky. He then moves an arm on the sextant to turn another mirror so that an image of the Sun or a particular star is seen in the telescope at the same level as the horizon. From the position of the arm against the scale on the sextant, he simply reads off the angle of the Sun or star. Knowing this angle and the correct time, the navigator can work out his position from special tables. Sextants are used in navigating ships and aircraft.

Below: Nowadays navigation is aided by radar. The radar aerial on a ship sends out radar waves, which are rather like radio waves. These waves are reflected by nearby objects and sent back towards the ship. The aerial picks up the returning waves and feeds them to a screen Above: like a television screen. On the screen a map-like picture of the ship's surroundings is displayed. From the radar picture, the captain of the ship can tell exactly where he is, even in thick fog. Radar is also extremely important in aircraft navigation.

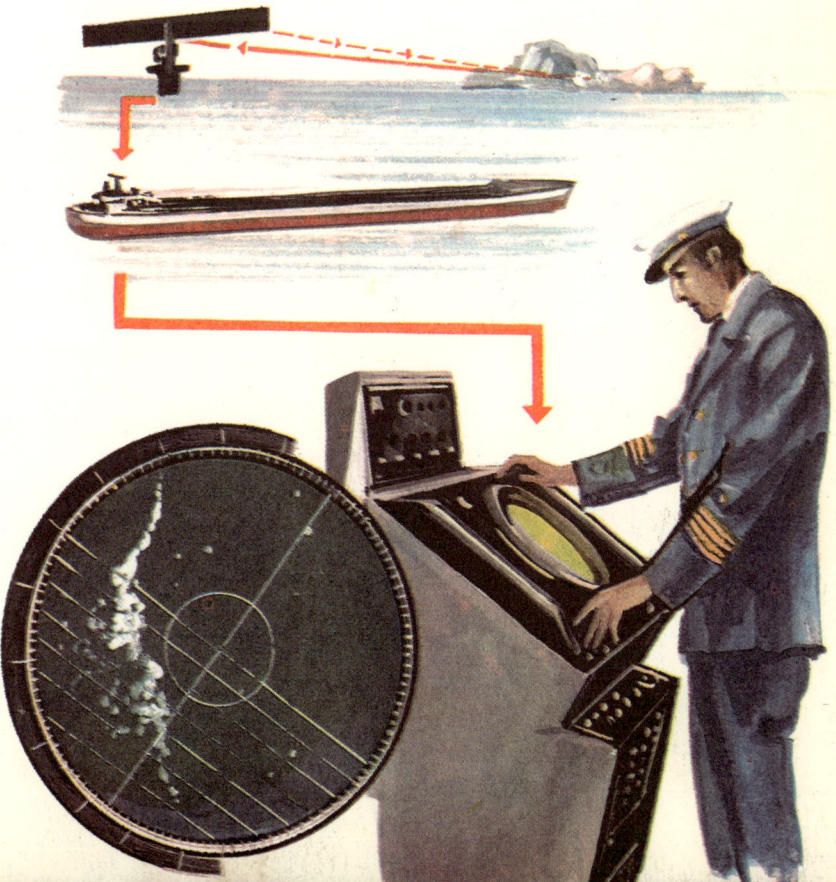

Telescopes Open Up the Universe

Until the early 1600s, astronomers had to rely upon their own unaided eyes to view the Universe. They could not see what the heavenly bodies look like but, with the aid of instruments like the quadrant, they were able to make very good star maps. These maps were vital in improving the calendar and perfecting navigation.

The invention of the telescope by a Dutch spectaclemaker called Hans Lippershey in 1608 revolutionized astronomy. By the following year, Galileo had a telescope and he immediately turned it to the heavens. He soon made many discoveries — the mountains and craters on the Moon, the moons of Jupiter, the phases of Venus and the sunspots on the Sun. He also observed the rings of Saturn, though his telescope was not quite powerful enough to show them clearly. His telescope still showed the stars as points of light, proving that they are very far away. As bigger and bigger telescopes were built, man began to look beyond the stars.

A giant telescope built by the astronomer Hevelius, a German astronomer of the 1600s. The telescope was made very long in an effort to overcome chromatic aberration, which causes coloured fringes to form around images. However, the instrument was very difficult to use and it was soon surpassed by the reflecting telescope designed by Sir Isaac Newton.

Above: These strange-shaped buildings are part of an observatory built in the 1700s near Jaipur in India. They were used for sighting stars so that their positions in the heavens could be accurately fixed.

Above: The oldest observatory on the American continent. It was built by the Maya Indians at the height of their empire and stood in their capital at Chichen Itza in Mexico.

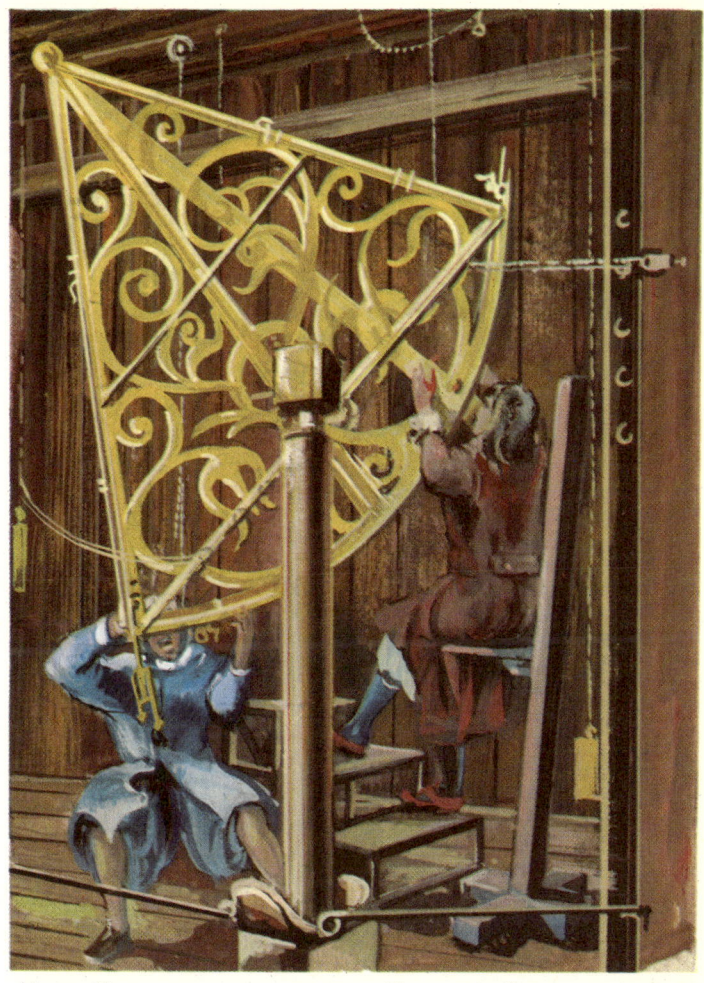

Above: Two astronomers use a primitive kind of sextant to measure the angle of the Sun above the horizon. Nowadays the sextant is much smaller and easier to use.

Below: It is very dangerous to look at the Sun through a telescope. The Sun's rays are concentrated by the telescope and can cause blindness. This fact must have been found out very soon after the invention of the telescope, and these astronomers are using the correct method of observing the Sun.

Above: The observatory at Greenwich, London. Built in 1675, it continued to make observations until after World War II. The Greenwich meridian, 0° longitude, passes through the observatory.

Probing the Depths of the Universe

To see distant stars and galaxies we need to use really big telescopes. This is not because we need a big telescope to obtain a larger image of the star or galaxy. Getting a high magnification is simply a matter of choosing more powerful lenses for the telescope. The reason is that a small telescope produces a faint image because it does not take in much light from the sky. A brighter image is needed to find out all there is to know about a star or galaxy. Wide telescopes must therefore be used to gather as much light as possible.

There are two basic kinds of telescopes — refracting telescopes and reflecting telescopes. Both telescopes first form an image of a heavenly body and then view this image with a magnifying lens. But the image is formed in different ways. In a refracting telescope, a lens like a magnifying glass is used to produce the image. In a reflecting telescope, a curved mirror like a shaving mirror is used instead of a lens. Refracting telescopes can only be built to a certain size, because lenses cannot be made very large. The largest refracting telescope is at Yerkes Observatory in the United States and has a lens just over one metre across. Mirrors can be made much larger than lenses and the largest reflecting telescope has a mirror 6 metres across. It is in the U.S.S.R.

These large telescopes are kept beneath domes in observatories which are built on the tops of high mountains far away from towns.

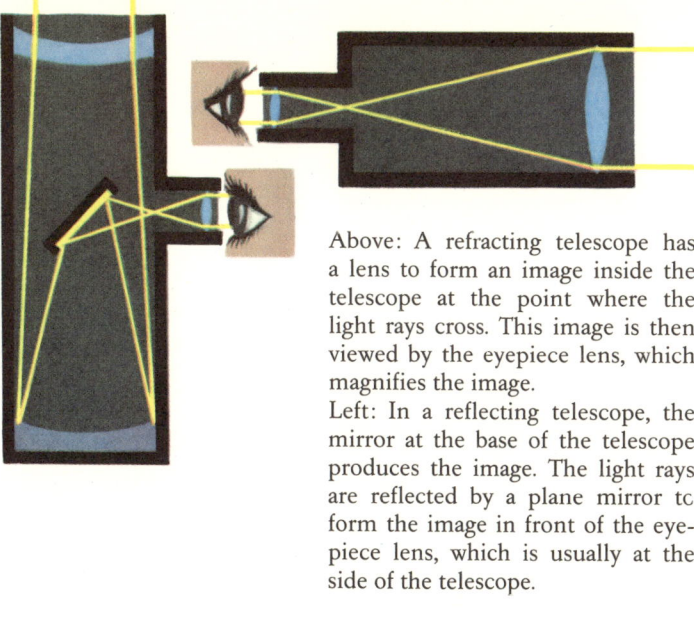

Above: A refracting telescope has a lens to form an image inside the telescope at the point where the light rays cross. This image is then viewed by the eyepiece lens, which magnifies the image.

Left: In a reflecting telescope, the mirror at the base of the telescope produces the image. The light rays are reflected by a plane mirror to form the image in front of the eyepiece lens, which is usually at the side of the telescope.

Below: The world's largest refracting telescope is at Yerkes Observatory in the United States. The main lens is 102 centimetres across.
Inset: Newton's first reflecting telescope. It was only 15 centimetres long, but it magnified about 40 times.

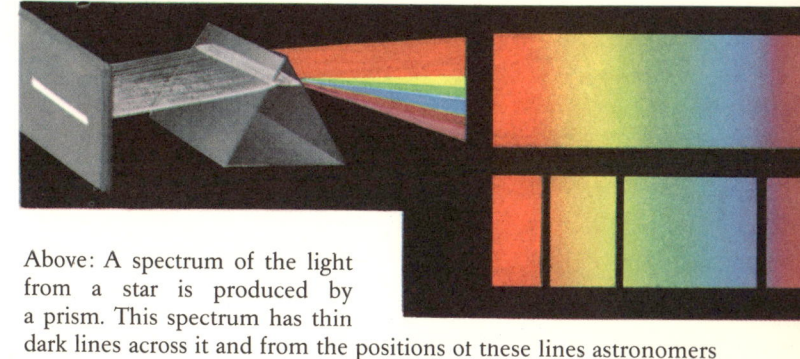

Above: A spectrum of the light from a star is produced by a prism. This spectrum has thin dark lines across it and from the positions of these lines astronomers can find which substances are present in a star.

Below: Apparatus for producing spectra of stars and galaxies is attached to the eyepiece of a telescope. In the case of galaxies, the spectrum obtained can also tell us how far away a galaxy is.

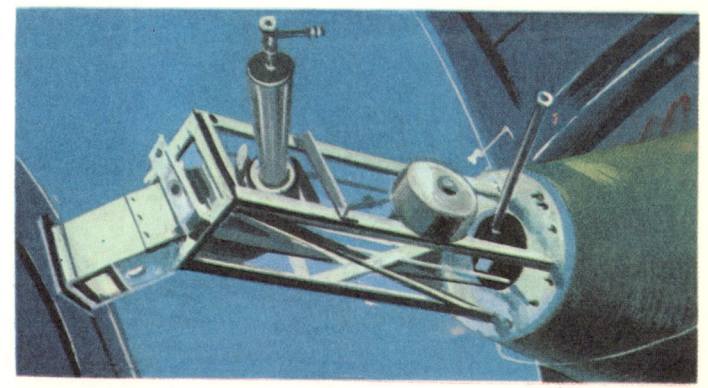

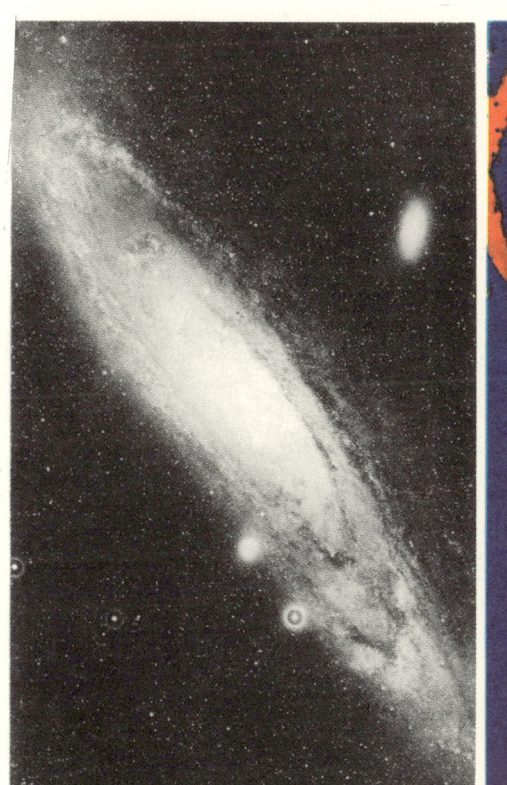

Opposite page: The great reflecting telescope at Mount Palomar in the United States. This telescope has a mirror just over 5 metres across, and it was the largest in the world before the Russian 6-metre instrument was built.

Above: Two photographs of the galaxy Andromeda. The picture on the left is a normal black-and-white photograph of the galaxy and shows what it looks like to the eye. The picture on the right is taken with invisible radiation and not with visible light. It shows more details of the structure of the galaxy.

Signals from Outer Space

Nearly everyone knows that the voices and music we hear on the radio come from a long way away. A large aerial at the radio station sends out radio waves through the air. The waves are invisible, but the aerial connected to a radio set picks them up and the radio set changes the waves into sound. Radio waves come through space to us from the Sun, the planet Jupiter, the stars and far-off galaxies. These radio signals are very weak and large aerials called radio telescopes are needed to pick them up. What radio astronomers hear is a hissing or crackling noise. But astronomers can find out much information about the Universe from the directions in which the signals are detected and from the strength of the signals.

There are two kinds of radio telescopes. One kind has a large bowl of metal struts and a small aerial at the centre of the bowl. The radio waves strike all parts of the bowl, and the bowl reflects the waves so that they all meet at the aerial. In this way the radio waves are increased in strength. In many instruments the bowl can be moved by large motors so that it faces any part of the sky. Some radio telescopes have huge, fixed bowls, but they cover a wide area of the sky because the Earth rotates and carries the telescope in a circle.

A radio telescope works by focusing radio waves (red arrows) from space at an aerial in the centre of a metal bowl. The signals received at the aerial then go to recording machines such as tape recorders and machines that trace out the signals on strips of paper.

Left: A recording instrument traces a line showing the strength of radio waves received by a radio telescope. The pen in the recorder moves to and fro as the waves come in and the paper moves beneath it. In this way, a wavy line is traced on the paper showing how the radio waves vary.

Above: People have often wondered if other living beings exist somewhere in the Universe, and whether we could communicate with them by radio. As it is impossible to know what language they would speak, we would have to send pictures. This could easily be done by transmitting signals that could be assembled to make a pattern. In the illustration on the left, a pattern of two different signals (denoted by m and s) shows a man. However, even a slight distortion of the signals (right) would make the pattern impossible to understand.

Below: The huge radio telescope at Arecibo in Puerto Rico has the largest bowl of any radio telescope in the world. It is 305 metres across. The bowl is built on the slopes of a large hollow in the ground and the receiving aerial is suspended above the centre of the bowl. This radio telescope can detect bodies at the known boundaries of the Universe.

Above: Radio telescopes are essential to spaceflight. Not only do they enable astronauts to communicate with the Earth, but they can also be used to find a spacecraft's position. The United States has a huge network of tracking stations around the world so that they can always be in touch with their spacecraft at any time of day or night.

The Greatest Mystery of All

As man has probed deeper and deeper into the Universe with great optical telescopes and with radio telescopes, he has made a bewildering number of discoveries. First he found that millions of other galaxies exist beside our own Galaxy of stars, and then he found that the galaxies are all rushing away from each other. He also discovered strange bodies in the skies, such as quasars, which seem to be very far away but must be unbelievably bright if they are. Quasars are a mystery, and so too are pulsars, newly-discovered stars that spin at great speed and are so heavy that they would weigh 100,000 times as much as the heaviest metal (if they could be weighed). Now space probes are reaching the limits of the Solar System (below) and making new discoveries, and satellites orbiting the Earth are detecting rays from space that we cannot receive on Earth. These satellites are finding more mysteries — such as the amazing black holes, which are thought to be regions of space that trap light rays within them so that they always remain dark.

But the greatest mystery of all is how the Universe formed. Astronomers know that the Universe is expanding, and many believe that long ago it may have been created by the explosion of some original body so that the galaxies formed have been rushing away from each other ever since. But how did this original body form in the first place? Perhaps the Universe will stop expanding one day and then start to contract. As the galaxies come together, a body like the original body would be formed again. Perhaps this would then explode again, starting a new cycle of expansion and contraction. Possibly these cycles could have been going on for ever, and will continue to go on for ever. But we may never know for sure.

Above: One of the many millions of galaxies that are to be seen throughout the Universe. Stars form as clouds of gas and dust floating in space condense and heat up. A galaxy forms as a group of stars condenses in the same region of space. Within a galaxy, new stars are still forming.

Left: Sometimes new stars appear in the sky. These stars are called novas or novae from *nova,* the Latin word for new. Tycho Brahe became the first known astronomer to record a nova. He found one in the constellation of Cassiopeia, as this old illustration shows. However, the Chinese are known to have seen a nova in the Crab constellation in 1054. In fact, these stars are not stars that suddenly form. They are faint stars that suddenly flare up in brightness. Novas are often detected by astronomers.

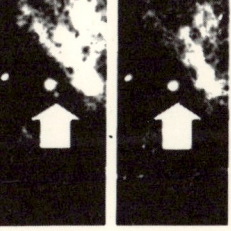

Above: A new kind of star was discovered in 1967, when radio astronomers detected a star that was producing regular signals or pulses of radio waves. The star was called a pulsar and astronomers wondered whether the signals were some kind of message from outer space because exactly the same number of pulses were produced every second. Two years after, a flashing star was found where another pulsar had been detected. The sequence of pictures shows it flashing on and off. This pulsar was found in the Crab Nebula and it is thought to be the remains of the star that exploded and became a supernova in 1054.

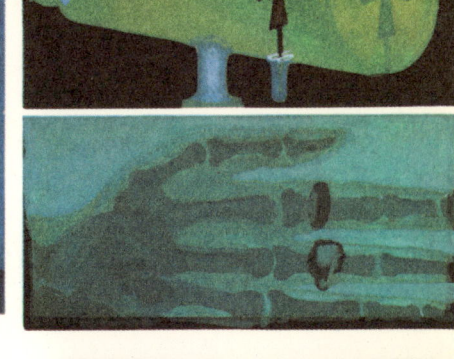

Above: A German physicist named Wilhelm Roentgen discovered X-rays in 1895. He found that invisible rays were produced by a cathode-ray tube (top right). The X-rays penetrate most materials and are used to examine the inside of the body (above right). In astronomy, special satellites orbiting the Earth are detecting the X-rays that come from the heavenly bodies, and making new discoveries about the Universe.

Above: Astronomers can solve the mysteries of the Universe only by detecting the various rays that come to the Earth from the heavenly bodies. Among the strangest of these rays are streams of very, very small particles called neutrinos. Most rays and particles are stopped by the Earth's atmosphere or by the ground, but most neutrinos pass right through the Earth! The only way they can be detected is to have special detectors at the bottom of deep mine-shafts, where no other rays or particles can penetrate. Astronomers believe that neutrinos are produced in stars, so detecting and measuring neutrinos should tell us more about how the stars shine.

Below: In the case of the Moon, man has been able to visit another world and bring back rocks and examine them in laboratories. The Moon missions have given us far more knowledge of the Moon than we could ever obtain just by observing it through telescopes.

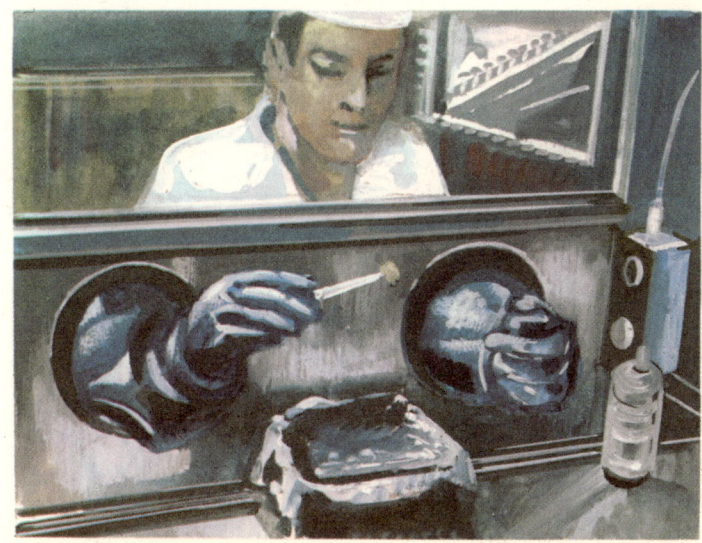

Destinies in the Stars?

Stars twinkle in the night sky. The town is in darkness, apart from a flicker of candlelight coming from the house of a well-known astrologer. Inside, the astrologer is busy trying to predict what is going to happen to his customers. The man with the big hat is perhaps a merchant and wants to know whether or not the stars promise him good luck in his business. And what of the couple who are standing by the door? What do they want from the astrologer? Perhaps they wish to know of their chances of making a happy marriage or whether they may expect any children.

All the people in the room believe that their destinies can be told from the positions of the stars. Most important is which sign they were born under — which of the twelve constellations of the zodiac is theirs. The astrologer is bent over his desk, intently making calculations with the aid of his books and the observations made by his assistants. He waits impatiently for them to tell him what they can see. Once he has made his calculations, he will assemble a horoscope for each of his customers. The horoscope is a chart showing the positions of the stars and planets in the heavens at the time of a person's birth. From the horoscope, the person's character and the main events of his life can be foretold.

Our scene took place many centuries ago, as you can tell by the costumes. Nowadays some astrologers do still manage to carry on a business, but few people now really believe that their lives are ruled by the stars from birth. What happens to people is thought to depend on the basic talents they inherit from their parents and on their upbringing and experiences in life.

Above: A stone-age man picks up a stone from the ground and tries to make out some meaning from the marks on it — perhaps the stone has some kind of message affecting his life. He must certainly take notice of the heavens, for the Sun deeply affects his livelihood.

Left: A medieval engraving shows an angel turning the sky around a city, which represents the Earth. The figures represent the planets in the sky. At the top we see Mars with a sword. Then come Mercury with the hand of a clock, Saturn with a scythe, the Moon shown as a woman with a crescent (for the Moon is always feminine), Jupiter, Venus, and finally the Sun. The picture is a horoscope depicting war because the god of war, Mars, stands over it.

Above: The signs of the zodiac were also connected with the body. This illustration divides up the body into twelve sections, each with a particular sign.

Above: By the Middle Ages, people in Europe no longer stood in fear of a sungod, and they no longer believed that comets signified disaster to come or that eclipses swallowed the Sun. However, they believed fervently that the positions of the stars and planets in the skies fixed the course of their lives.

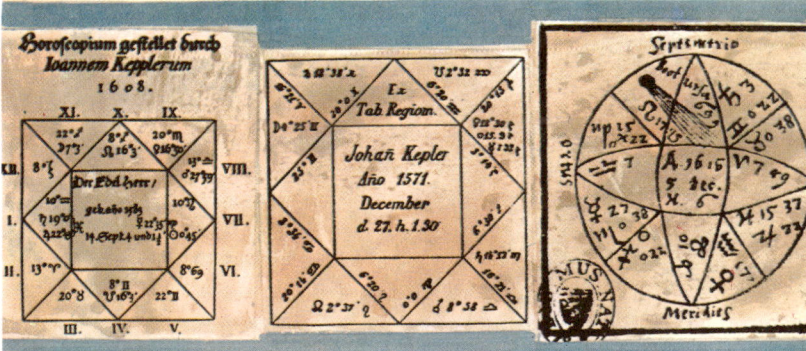

Above: Three horoscopes. On the left is a horoscope made by the astronomer Johann Kepler, who was also a keen astrologer. During his lifetime he was valued more highly as an astrologer than as an astronomer. This horoscope was made for the German general, Wallenstein, who was also a firm believer in astrology. The horoscope shows the positions of the planets and constellations of the zodiac at a particular time in Wallenstein's life. In the centre is Kepler's own horoscope for the day and hour of his birth. To the right is another horoscope of unknown origin; it is interesting as it shows a comet crossing the zodiac.

Below: An old picture snowing the association of the signs of the zodiac with particular parts of the body. For example, Gemini (the twins) is associated with the arms, and Aries (the ram) with the head.

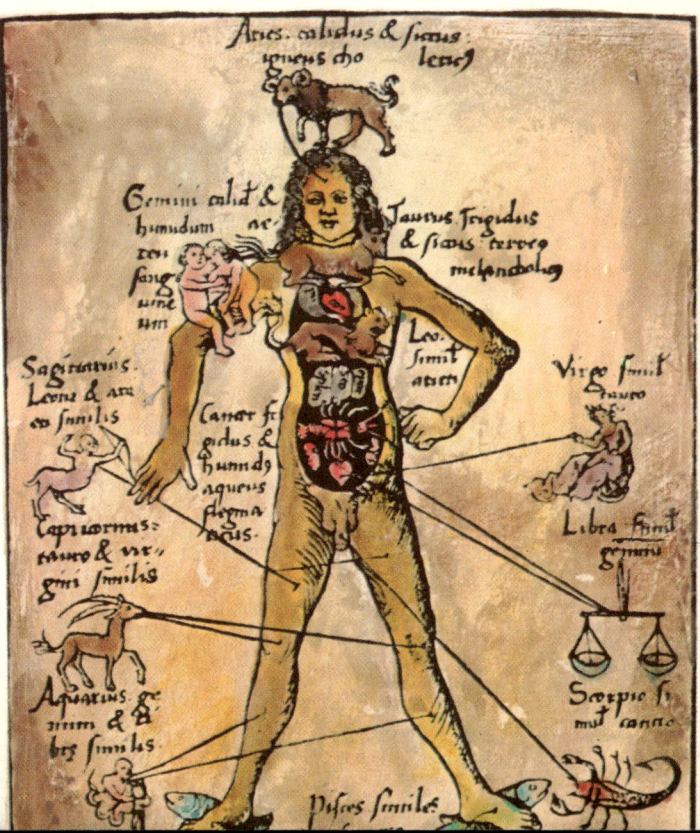

The Power of Reaction

In the first century AD, there lived in the city of Alexandria a Greek engineer named Hero. Hero made a brilliant discovery that could have changed all our lives. He made a hollow sphere that could spin in a frame, attached two bent tubes to the sphere and filled it with water. He then lit a fire under the sphere and, when the water boiled, it began to spin as jets of steam spouted from the tubes. Hero's device was a way of converting steam power to motion. It was only used as a toy, but had it been developed into a powerful steam engine, then it would have changed the course of history.

Hero's device is like a lawn sprinkler, which uses jets of water instead of steam. It works by the principle of action and reaction, which was not understood until Sir Isaac Newton made it one of his laws of motion. The law simply states that to every ac-

tion, there is an equal and opposite reaction. You can understand this if you think of yourself standing on a trolley or cart, and then jumping off. As you jump, you move forward but you must push your feet against the trolley to launch yourself forward. As a result, the trolley moves backward. Both you and the trolley move with an equal force in opposite directions; the force with which you move forward is called the *action* and the force with which the trolley moves backward is the *reaction*.

Modern forms of transport work by reaction. An aircraft forces out a jet of air from its engines and moves forward as the jet of air moves backward. Rockets are another example. In this case, the rocket engine forces out hot gases as it burns its fuel. A jet engine cannot work in space because it needs air to burn its fuel. But a rocket carries its own supply of oxygen instead of air and so can work in space where there is no air. For this reason, and because they can be very powerful, rockets are used to power spacecraft and missiles.

1. Hero of Alexandria and his steam engine.
2. A cuttlefish moves forward (red arrow) by squirting a jet of water backward (blue arrow).
3. A Chinese rocket launcher.
4. A European rocket launcher.
5. A rocket-powered racing car.

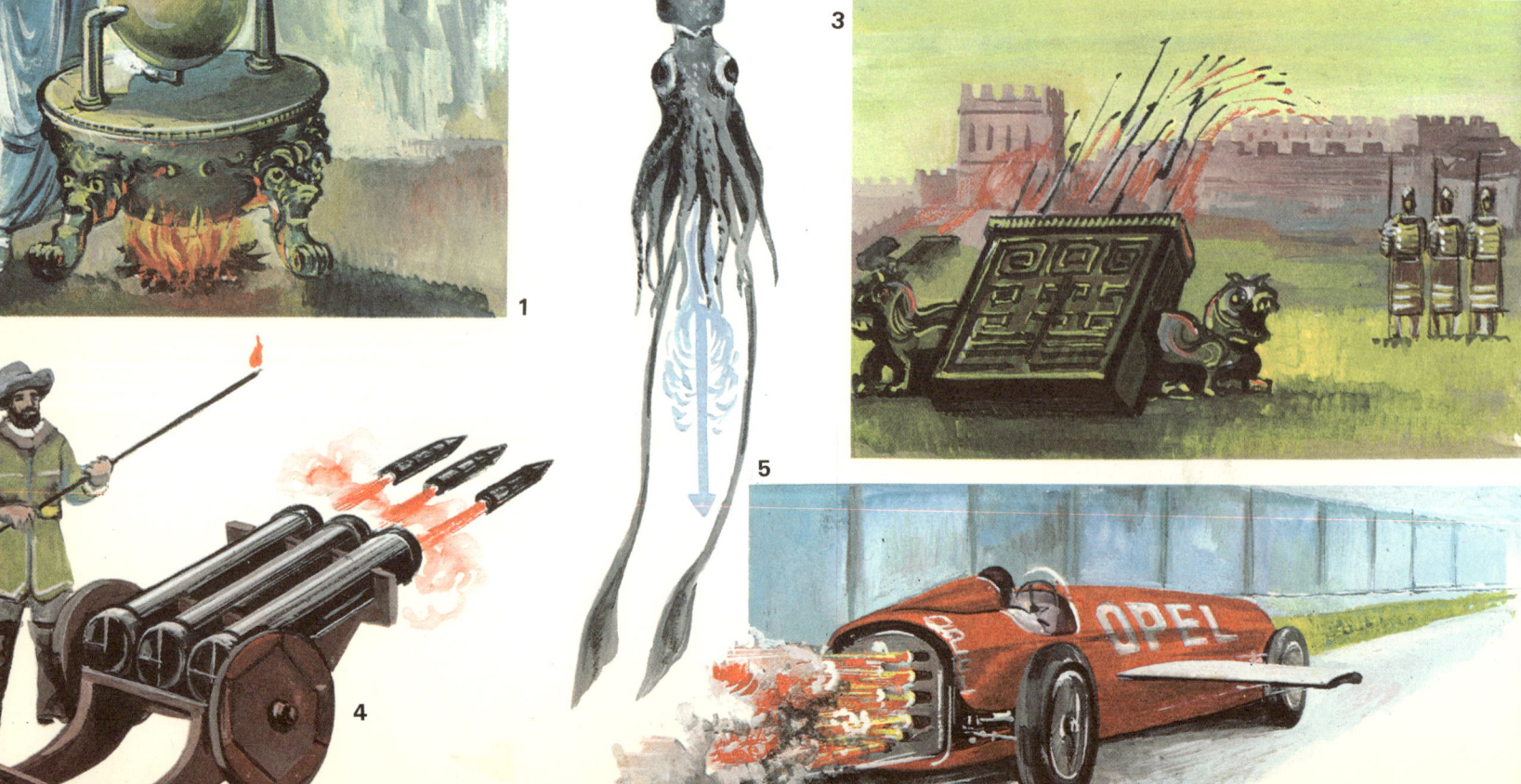

Above: Konstantin Tsiolkovsky, who lived in Russia from 1857 to 1935, began to think about spaceflight twenty years before the first aircraft flew. He realized that rockets would be needed and correctly predicted the kind of fuels they would use. He also believed that a space rocket would have to work in several separate stages — an essential method for spaceflight.

Right: Reinhold Tilling experimented with solid-fuelled rockets from 1928 to 1933. Most of today's smaller space rockets contain solid fuels. Tilling gave his rockets wings. On reaching the highest point of ist climb these were extended so that the rocket could glide back to Earth.

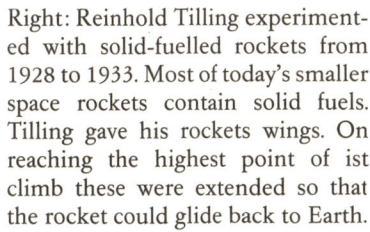

Above: Robert H. Goddard was the practical pioneer of the space rocket. He built and tested the first liquid-fuel rocket in 1926, and it reached a speed of 100 kilometres an hour. By 1935, Goddard's rockets were achieving speeds of 1000 kilometres an hour. But the United States Government did not support his work and Goddard was unable to develop his rockets any further.

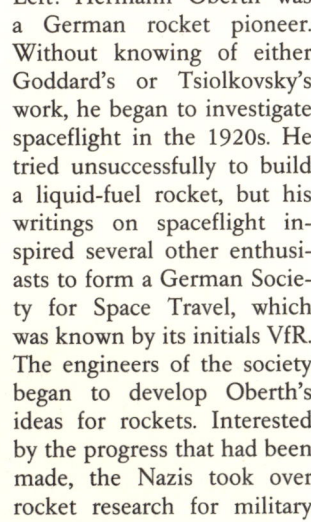
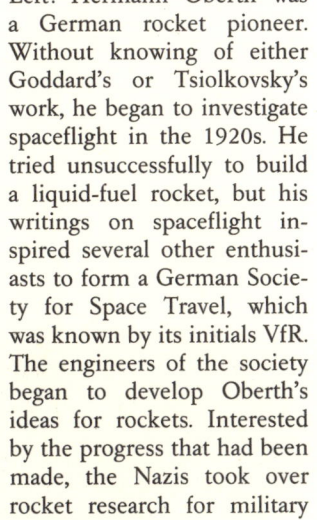

Left: Hermann Oberth was a German rocket pioneer. Without knowing of either Goddard's or Tsiolkovsky's work, he began to investigate spaceflight in the 1920s. He tried unsuccessfully to build a liquid-fuel rocket, but his writings on spaceflight inspired several other enthusiasts to form a German Society for Space Travel, which was known by its initials VfR. The engineers of the society began to develop Oberth's ideas for rockets. Interested by the progress that had been made, the Nazis took over rocket research for military purposes.

Above: Wernher von Braun was one of the leading members of the VfR, the German rocket society. He soon surpassed Goddard's achievements and continued to develop rockets when World War II came. During the war the Nazis built two kinds of missiles. The V1 (top) was powered by a ram jet, an early form of jet engine. It was armed with explosives that blew up when the missile fell to the ground. The V2 (right), was another rocket developed by Von Braun. After the war. Von Braun went to the United States where he developed the V2 into the mighty Saturn rockets that launched the Apollo manned spacecraft to the Moon.

Gravity — The Force that Brings Us Down to Earth

If you drop something, it falls to the ground. This is such an everyday happening that it was a long time before anyone asked *why* this should happen. However, Sir Isaac Newton asked himself this question when he saw an apple fall from a tree. He reasoned that the Earth must have a force that always pulls us down to the ground. He called the force gravity, and he went on to say that every object has gravity. The force always acts between any two bodies, pulling them together. However, the greater the object is, the more gravity it has. Therefore, a bigger object will pull a smaller one towards it. In everyday terms, the two bodies are ourselves and the Earth, which is very much bigger than we are. Therefore, we are pulled by gravity to the ground. The force of gravity acts towards the centre of a body, so that every object on the surface of the Earth is pulled down towards its centre. The floor or ground stops us falling to the centre, of course. The force of gravity between two bodies gets less as they get farther apart, but you would have to travel many millions of miles out into space before you could entirely get away from gravity. Why then do spacemen become weightless when they are in orbit? People often suppose that this is because the astronauts have left the Earth's gravity, but this is not true. We all have weight because the floor or ground is stopping us from falling to the centre of the Earth. We stand on some scales, and the scales register the force with which we push down on them as our weight. However, when a spacecraft is moving through space, the Earth's gravity always acts on it, either slowing it down or speeding it up or keeping it in orbit. Both the spacecraft and everything inside it are being pulled by the Earth. The astronauts cannot fall towards the floor of the spacecraft because the floor is always moving in exactly the same way as they are. They therefore have no weight, and float in mid-air unless they are tethered to their seats.

Left: Everyone standing on the Earth is pulled by gravity towards its centre. This is why people on the opposite sides of the Earth are upside-down to each other, but all feel that they are standing upright.

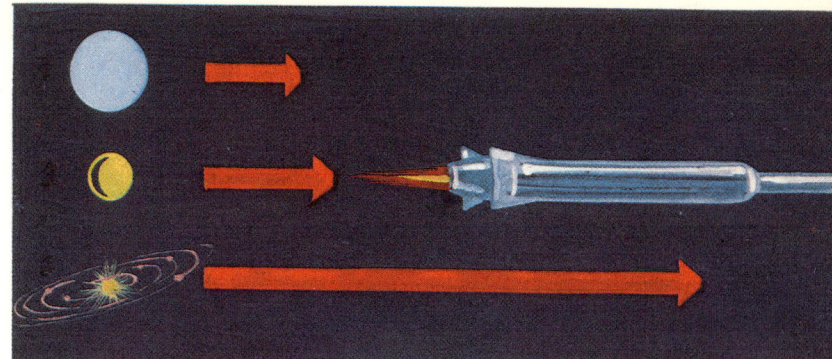

Above: A spacecraft must reach a certain speed before it can make a journey into space. If it does not go fast enough, it will sooner or later fall back to Earth. To achieve orbit round the Earth (top), the spacecraft must be launched above the atmosphere and given a speed of 8 kilometres a second. It will then continue to circle the Earth without falling to the ground. To get to the Moon or planets, a higher speed of 11 kilometres a second is needed (centre). If it does not travel at this speed, the spacecraft will either fall back to Earth or go into orbit around it. To leave the Solar System, the vast speed of 42 kilometres per second would be needed (bottom), because the Solar System has a greater force of gravity than the Earth.

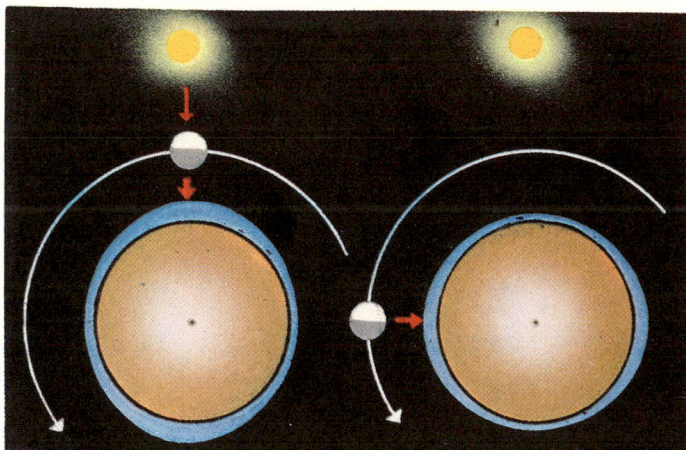

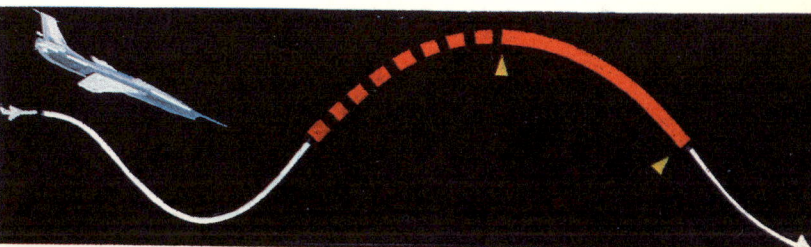

Above: Gravity causes the tides. The gravitational fields of the Moon and Sun act on the Earth, attracting the waters of the ocean towards them and causing them to rise by a few metres. The motion of the Earth also causes a rise to occur on the opposite side of the Earth. Between the two rises in level are two falls in level. As the Earth rotates, it passes through both rises and both falls in one day, producing two high tides (bottom) and two low tides (centre). The rise and fall is greatest when the Moon and Sun are in line with the Earth; this occurs once a month and gives the spring tide (top left). The neap tide occurs between two spring tides, and happens when the Sun and Moon are at right-angles with the Earth (top right).

Above: Astronauts practise being weightless by taking special aircraft flights. The aircraft makes a steep climb and then cuts out its engines. It continues to climb and then falls (red lines in top picture) before starting the engines once more. During its unpowered flight, the aircraft and its occupants become weightless (bottom).

The Most Unusual Job in the World

Very few people are lucky enough to fly in space. Since manned spaceflight began in 1961, just over a hundred people have journeyed beyond the Earth's atmosphere. Of these, only one has been a woman. A dozen men have been to the Moon. At present, you have to be American or Russian to make a spaceflight, for no other countries have manned space programmes. However, these restrictions should disappear in the 1980s, when the space shuttle comes into operation.

Being an astronaut is a risky business, but not as dangerous as people once thought it would be. It is certainly a hard job to have. On a spaceflight, the occupants undergo terrific strain at the launch and before landing, when they weigh several times their own weight for about 10 minutes or so. For the rest of the voyage they are weightless. Yet, they must all the time perform difficult tasks.

An astronaut must be intelligent and in excellent physical and mental health; he must be courageous but not foolishly brave; he must have quick reactions and he must be able to keep his head in any situation. If a person has these qualities, then he may be selected to start training as an astronaut. This training takes several years.

The astronaut is given a good training in navigation and in the use of all the many kinds of instruments and equipment needed for spaceflight. He must spend many hours practising his mission in simulators. These are machines that give the astronaut the same kinds of conditions that he will experience in space. He is whirled round inside a giant centrifuge (below), so that his weight increases several times, just as it does at launch and before landing. Weightlessness can be experienced in an aircraft (see page 47). The astronaut must also learn how to survive in all kinds of conditions on Earth, in case he crashes far from civilization.

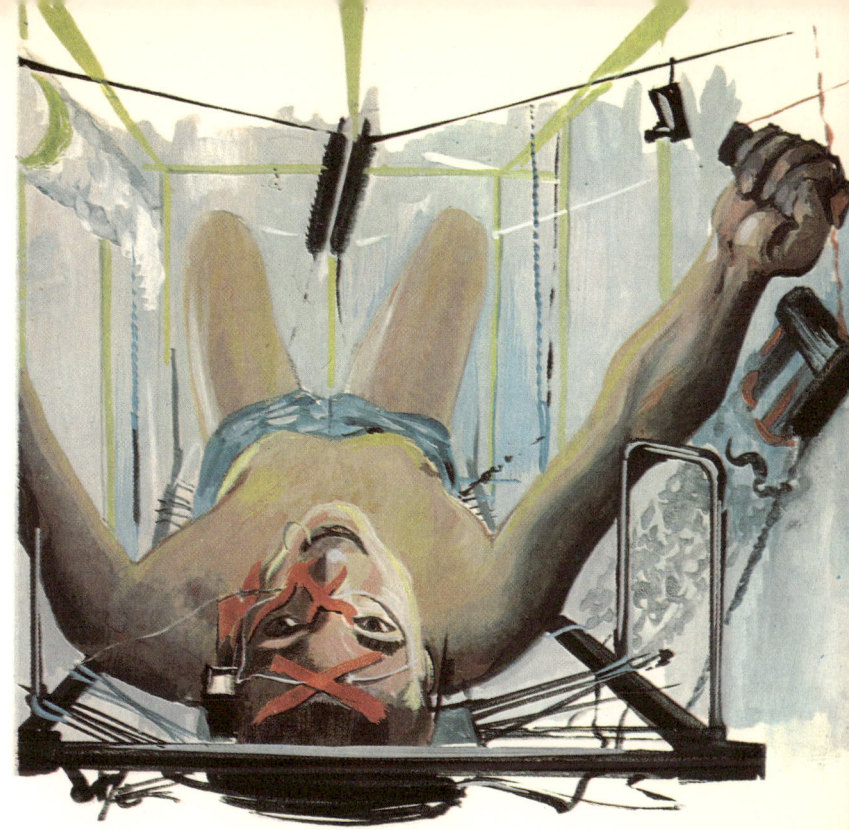

Above: In planning a spacecraft, the designer must make sure that all the controls in the cabin will be within the reach of the astronauts. He must remember that the astronauts will be wearing their space-suits and will be strapped into their seats for part of the spaceflight. Here, a model of a cabin in the first design stages is being tested.

Above: Doctors check the physical health of a team of astronauts very carefully. Here, a trainee astronaut is undergoing a test while instruments are connected to him. From the readings on the instruments, the doctors can tell whether or not the man will be able to stand up to the harsh conditions of spaceflight.

Below: In this test, the astronaut has to ride a bicycle. The machine is supported off the ground, so that it does not move. It is in fact a device to make the astronaut do a certain amount of work. As he works, the doctors check his heartbeat and blood pressure. He wears a sealed spacesuit, as he would during a Moon walk, and the doctors check his breathing by measuring the amount of oxygen he uses. In this way, they can find out if the man uses the correct amount of oxygen to perform a certain amount of work.

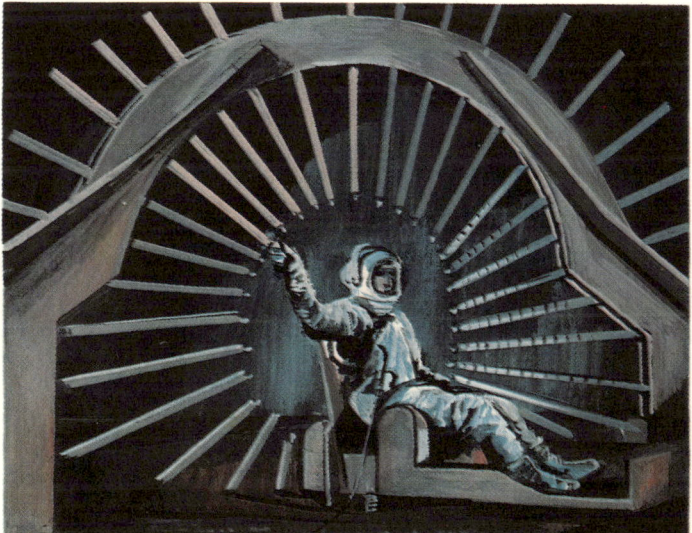

Above: An astronaut practises his space mission in a simulator. The simulator is a full-size model of the cabin of the spacecraft. As the astronaut, dressed in his spacesuit if necessary, operates the controls and equipment in the cabin, the instruments respond as if a real spaceflight were taking place. In this way, the astronaut gets to know how to handle his craft so thoroughly that his actions become almost automatic. The simulator can tilt in all directions (red arrows) because the spacecraft will do so. The astronaut must be able to keep complete control over his craft even though he may appear to be upside-down or on his side.

Highlights of the Space Age

The space age began on 4 October 1957, when the first satellite was launched into space from the U.S.S.R. It was called Sputnik 1, and the bleep-bleep of its radio gave man the first information he gathered in space. Aboard Sputnik 2, launched on 3 November 1957, was a dog called Laika, the first animal in space. She blazed a trail in space for man to follow.

Man entered space for the first time on 12 April 1961 with the flight of Yuri Gagarin once around the Earth aboard the Russian spacecraft Vostok 1. The Americans soon followed when John Glenn made the first American orbital flight on 20 February 1962. A space race followed. At first the Russians drew ahead, but soon the Americans caught up. On 21 July 1969, during the Apollo 11 mission, the American astronauts Neil Armstrong and Edwin Aldrin became the first men to set foot on the Moon. Five more American landings followed.

The longest flights were made with the three Skylab missions of 1973 and 1974. Astronauts and scientists worked aboard the Skylab space station in orbit around the Earth. The crew of the Skylab 3 mission stayed in space for a record 84 days.

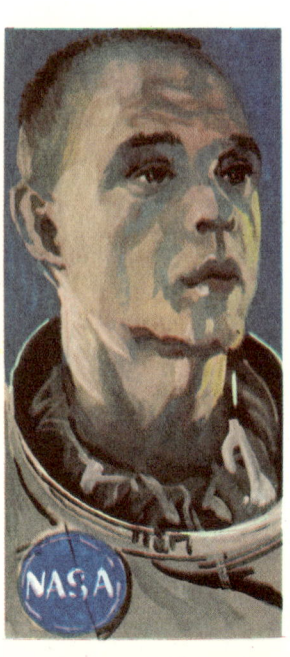

Above: The first man in space was a Russian cosmonaut, Yuri Gagarin. Right: John Glenn, the first American to orbit the Earth.

Below: The scene of the Moon first landing reflected in a space helmet.

Above: Valentina Tereshkova, the first woman in space, flew aboard the Russian craft Vostok 6 in 1963.

Above: Alexei Leonov made the first space walk in 1965. He floated outside his craft for 20 minutes.

Neil Armstrong   Michael Collins   Edwin Aldrin

Above: Armstrong and Aldrin landed on the Moon in July 1969. Collins orbited the Moon. Left: An astronaut's boot makes a footprint in some Moon dust.

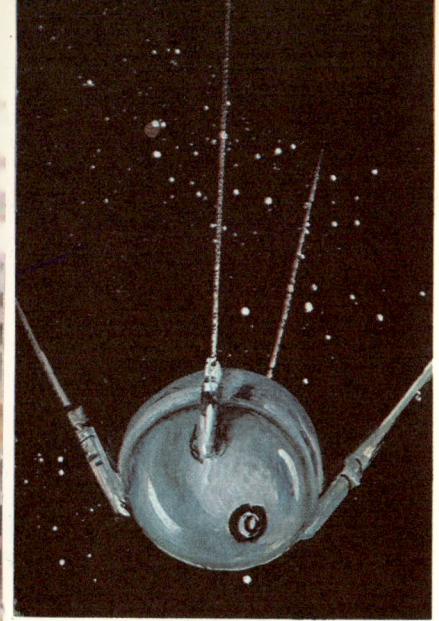

Left: Man placed his first satellite in space on 4 October 1957. It was the Russian satellite Sputnik 1. The satellite measured 58 cm in diameter and weighed 84 kilograms. Sputnik 1 radioed information about conditions in space back to Earth until its batteries gave out three weeks later.

Above: An American astronaut floats in space outside his spacecraft. As there is no air on the Moon, the astronauts had to wear their spacesuits as they worked. Space walks like this one took place before the landing on the Moon so that astronauts could find out what it would be like working in space. During a space walk, the astronaut is tethered to the spacecraft by a long line.

Above: Two Gemini spacecraft meet in space. To get to the Moon, it was necessary to develop ways for two spacecraft to find each other in space and then fasten together. This technique is called 'rendezvous and docking', and it was perfected during the American Gemini missions in 1965 and 1966.

Below: The first meeting in space of two spacecraft from different countries takes place as an American Apollo spacecraft (right) meets a Russian Soyuz spacecraft (left). If two different spacecraft can dock together, then stranded astronauts will have a greater chance of being rescued from space.

Above: Several animals made pioneering spaceflights before man ventured into space. The first animal to orbit the Earth was a Russian dog called Laika (top). She was launched aboard the satellite Sputnik 2 in 1957 and scientists checked her reactions to space travel by radio. The first American animal to orbit the Earth was a chimpanzee named Enos (bottom). He made his spaceflight in 1961. Laika did not return from space, as the Sputnik could not re-enter the atmosphere. Enos was luckier, for his Mercury spacecraft safely returned to the ground after two orbits of the Earth.

Rockets — The Most Powerful Vehicles of All

Only one kind of transport has enough power to launch a spacecraft — the rocket.

The spacecraft itself — the machine that carries the instruments or men that are to perform a space mission — is comparatively small and low-powered. It has to be fired into space with sufficient speed to enable it to orbit the Earth, or to get to the Moon or planets, so as to carry out its mission. The speeds are enormous — 11 kilometres a second to reach the Moon, for example. To launch a manned spacecraft to the Moon therefore needs a huge rocket.

The Moon rocket, called Saturn V, stands 111 metres high, including the Apollo spacecraft and an escape rocket on top. Its engines produce the power of about fifty jumbo jets as it leaves the ground. Although most of the Saturn V rocket consists of fuel, its metal casing and engines are also heavy. There is no point in carrying all this metal to the Moon if it is not to be used. Therefore, every unneeded part of the rocket, and of the spacecraft too, is thrown away as soon as it has been used. To do this saves fuel. This is why a huge rocket leaves the Earth at the beginning of a space mission, and a tiny spacecraft is all that returns. All the rest has been thrown away during the voyage.

Some space rockets are shown below. Those marked CCCP are Russian. Russia is believed to have a new rocket even more powerful than Saturn V.

Above: A Russian rocket about to fire. The gantries surrounding the rocket tilt back before launch.

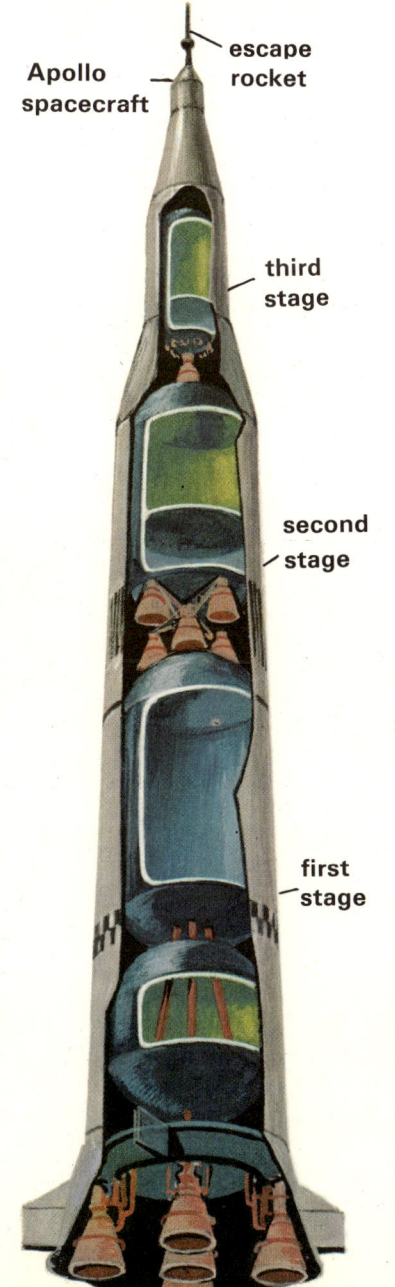

Apollo spacecraft — escape rocket

third stage

second stage

first stage

Above: The Kennedy space centre at Cape Canaveral in Florida in the United States. A Saturn V Moon rocket can be seen leaving the vehicle assembly building. The rocket crawls to its launching pad on a special transporter with caterpillar tracks. This crawler is the largest vehicle in the world. The Saturn rocket is held in a framework called a gantry. The arms of the gantry move back just before launch.

Left: A cross-section through a Saturn V Moon rocket. This rocket, like all space rockets, is made up of several stages, or smaller rockets, mounted on top of each other. As each stage uses up its fuel, it is released and the engine in the next stage fires. Finally, when all the stages have fired, the Apollo spacecraft is well on its way to the Moon. The stages either return to Earth by parachute, burn up in the atmosphere, or are lost in space.

Right: A cross-section of a liquid-fuel rocket. The two fuels are stored in separate tanks. In large rockets, one is usually kerosene or liquid hydrogen, and the other is liquid oxygen. Both liquids are pumped to the combustion chamber, where they are ignited. The kerosene or hydrogen burns fiercely with the oxygen, producing hot gases that rush at great speed from the exhaust (small arrow). As they do so, they push against the rest of the combustion chamber, and force the rocket forward (large arrow). Small rockets are similar in principle, although they use other fuels. The fuels may simply be forced into the combustion chamber by high-pressure gas from a chamber above the fuel tanks, as shown here. Often they ignite as they meet.

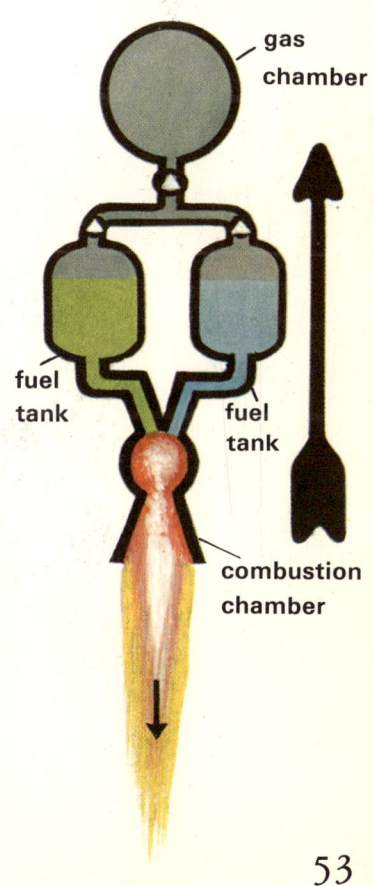

gas chamber

fuel tank

fuel tank

combustion chamber

Man on the Moon

It was only seven years after the first American orbited the Earth that men landed on the Moon. In this time there were four one-man Mercury flights, ten two-man Gemini flights and then four three-man Apollo test flights. All these flights showed that the Apollo spacecraft could safely get men to the Moon and back.

The first six Apollo flights were unmanned. The Apollo 7 to Apollo 10 missions were the test flights, and so the first Moon landing mission was Apollo 11. Two of the astronauts, Neil Armstrong and Edwin Aldrin, stepped on to the Moon's surface on 21 July 1969. Armstrong made the historic saying

'That's one small step for a man, one giant leap for mankind', and the two men gathered rocks and set up experiments for 2½ hours before returning to the lunar module.

There were five more Apollo spaceflights to the Moon. On the last one, Apollo 17 in December 1972, the two astronauts spent 22 hours working on the Moon. On the last three landings, the astronauts made several journeys away from the lunar module aboard a Moon car (below).

The crew of Apollo 13 had a lucky escape when part of their spacecraft exploded. They abandoned the Moon landing and returned safely to Earth.

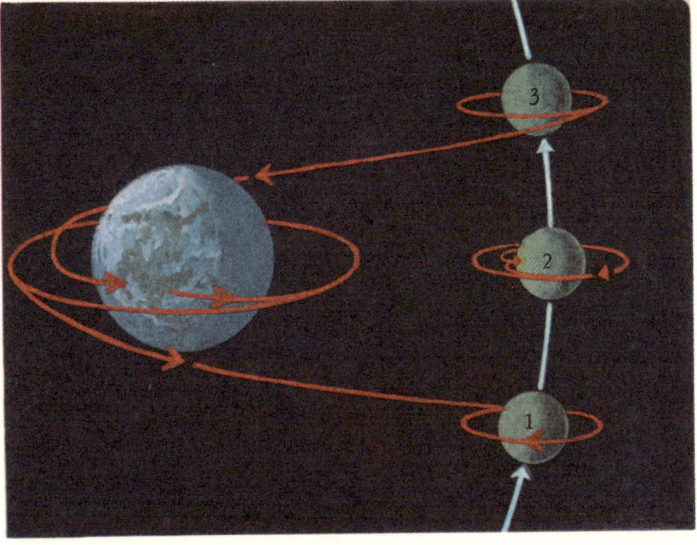

Above: The Apollo spacecraft flew to the Moon and back by a method called lunar orbit rendezvous. The Saturn V rocket launched this spacecraft first into Earth orbit and then towards the Moon. When the craft neared the Moon, it went into orbit. The lunar module then separated and descended to the surface. This module brought the crew back from the Moon and rejoined the rest of the Apollo spacecraft in Moon orbit before the return to Earth.

Below: The Apollo missions ended when the command module splashed down into the ocean beneath parachutes. The lunar module and service module were jettisoned before reaching Earth. A ship always stood near the splashdown point to take on the astronauts.

Above: The Russians did not attempt to send men to the Moon. Instead, they used automatic space probes to explore the Moon. One of these was the Lunokhod Moon walker. This machine was lowered by rockets to the Moon's surface, and then it trundled around the Moon, sending television pictures back to Earth and examining the surface and sending information back by radio. The Russians also used special space probes that landed on the Moon, scooped up some Moon rocks, and returned to Earth with them. However, they gained less information about the Moon than the Americans did with their manned landings.

Right: A piece of Moon rock brought back from the Moon by the Apollo astronauts. The minerals in the rock are similar to those in Earth rocks. Many of the Moon rocks and soil particles were glassy, because they were formed by great heat when meteorites crashed into the Moon.

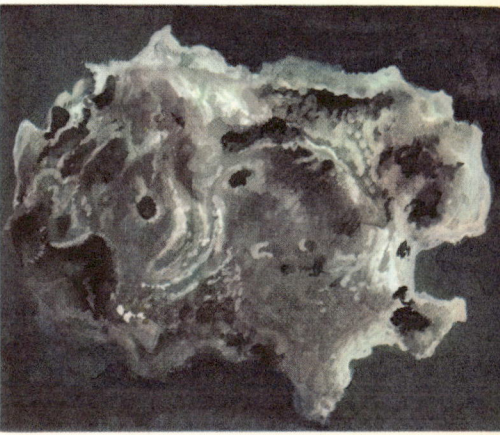

Left: The Apollo lunar module seen in orbit around the Moon. The Earth hangs like a great crescent in the sky.

Below: A century before the Moon landings, Jules Verne wrote a famous pair of stories called *From the Earth to the Moon* and *Round the Moon*. The stories were remarkable predictions of the Apollo spaceflights. The spacecraft was shell-shaped, not unlike the conical Apollo command module; it was launched from Florida, just as Apollo was; the spacemen orbited the Moon and were weightless during their flight; and they ended their flight by splashing down into the ocean near a ship, exactly as with the Apollo missions. This illustration of the splashdown is from the original edition of the book.

Man-made Moons in the Heavens

For millions of years, the Moon circled the Earth alone. Unlike the moons of the giant planets, it had no companions as it journeyed through space. Then, in 1957, it found itself with a neighbour when Sputnik 1 orbited the Earth too. Now there are hundreds of artificial satellites orbiting the Earth. These satellites can often be seen, slowly crossing the night sky like a wandering star.

Artificial satellites have many purposes. Some are scientific satellites. They make observations of the heavens and of the Earth, and radio their results back to Earth. Astronomers do not get completely clear pictures of the stars through telescopes because the atmosphere distorts images. With satellites, they can get much better results and they can also detect rays such as X-rays that come from space but do not penetrate the atmosphere as light rays do. The satellites also examine the magnetic field and radiation belts around the Earth. Many satellites photograph the Earth by different kinds of rays; their pictures can show up many things — such as pollution, diseased crops, shoals of fish and minerals — that we cannot easily see here on Earth. Communications satellites link continents. Telephone calls and television programmes go from one side of the world to another via radio links connecting us to the satellites. Weather satellites look down at the Earth and photograph the clouds and measure its heat. From these observations, weather men can make better forecasts of the world's weather. With satellites, they can see a hurricane far out to sea before it is detected on Earth; they warn people on the coast that it is approaching so that they have time to escape (below). Military satellites look down from space and can spot whether any nation is preparing to make war. Our man-made moons are proving a valuable aid to man in many ways.

Earth is not the only world with artificial satellites. Several are circling the Moon and Mars, taking pictures of the surfaces of these worlds.

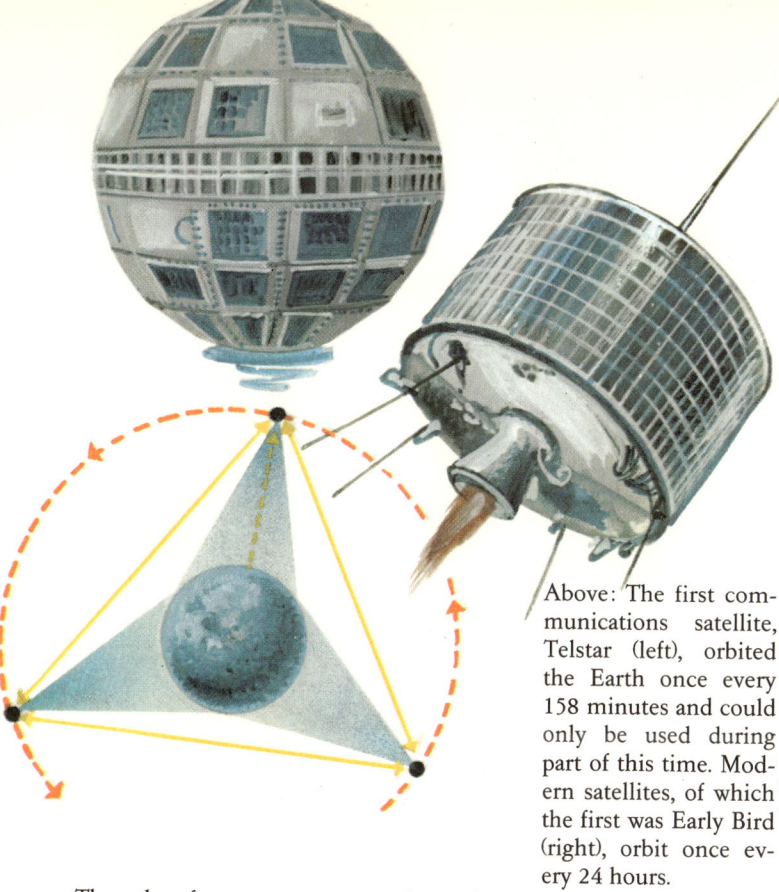

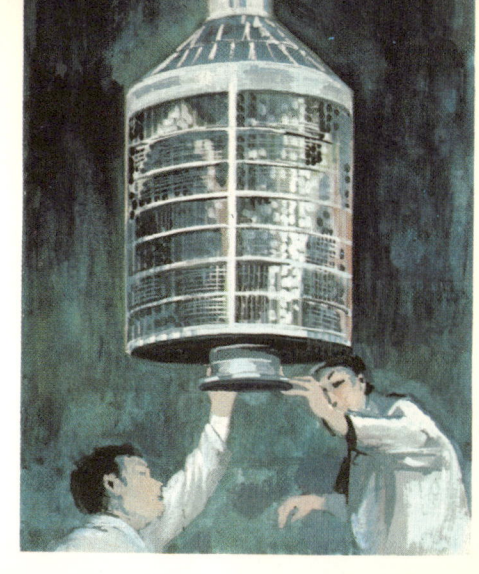

Right: Azur, a German satellite designed to make observations of the heavens from space. A few countries, including Britain, France, China and Japan, have put satellites into orbit with their own rockets. Most satellites are launched by American or Russian rockets.

Above: The first communications satellite, Telstar (left), orbited the Earth once every 158 minutes and could only be used during part of this time. Modern satellites, of which the first was Early Bird (right), orbit once every 24 hours.

They therefore appear to stay above the same point on the Earth. Three of these satellites can give complete world coverage communications.

Below: Molniya, a Russian communications satellite. The satellite has wings of solar cells that turn sunlight into electricity. The two radio aerials point to two different radio stations on Earth.

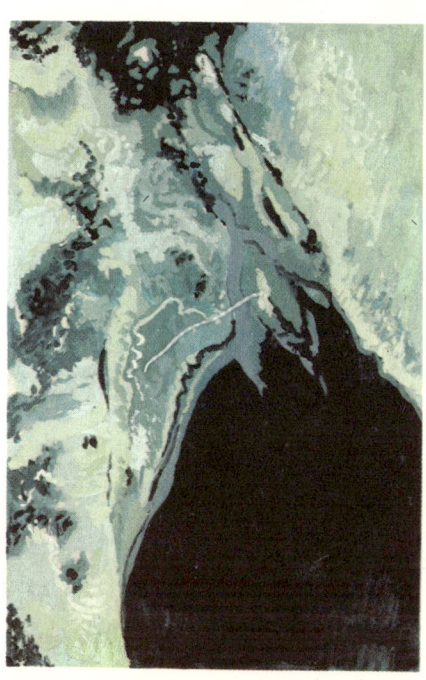

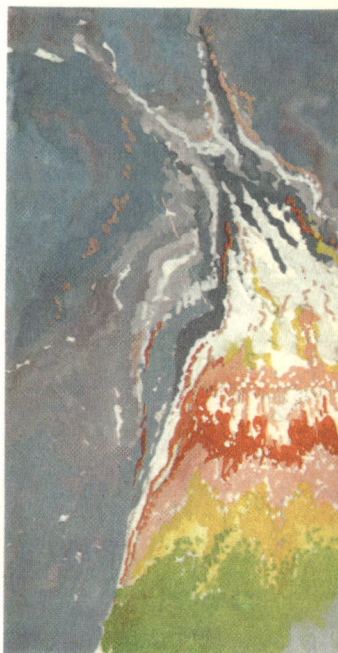

Above: Two pictures received from a satellite orbiting the Earth. On the left is a picture taken by normal light, showing a view of a river mouth from space. To the right is the same view taken by invisible infra-red rays and developed as a colour picture. The different colours form where different amounts of rays come from the Earth below, and they show up the currents flowing in the water.

Below: The Skylab space station was sent into orbit around the Earth by the USA in 1973. Three teams of astronauts visited Skylab for long periods, the longest being 84 days. The astronauts made observations of the Sun, stars and the Earth, and they conducted experiments in the weightless conditions aboard the space station. Each team used an Apollo spacecraft, shown docked to Skylab, to reach the station and return to Earth.

The Air Around Us

Modern man has little control over the weather, even though he understands how the weather works. But he is able to forecast the weather and knowing the weather that is to come, he can make decisions about when to harvest crops, for example. Although weather forecasting is not yet perfect, it has improved greatly in the last few years. This has happened for two reasons. One is that satellites now send us photographs of the Earth so that weather men can see the world's weather at a glance. The other reason is that the development of computers has enabled them to handle all the information provided by the satellites and make a good forecast quickly. Without computers, the weather would come and go long before the forecast could be worked out.

The patterns of weather around the world are caused mainly by the patterns of winds that blow over land and sea. A wind blowing over an ocean will pick up moisture as it goes. When it arrives over the land, it will tend to drop its moisture as rain. Knowing the directions of the winds is therefore vital to forecasting the weather. So too is the temperature, for hot air can hold more moisture before it sheds it as rain than cold air. Measuring the air pressure is also important, for winds blow from a region of high pressure to one of low pressure.

Left: The Earth receives heat from the Sun. At the Equator, directly beneath the Sun, it is hot because the Sun's rays are concentrated together. At the Poles, the rays are more spread out because the surface of the Earth slopes away from the Sun, and it is cold.

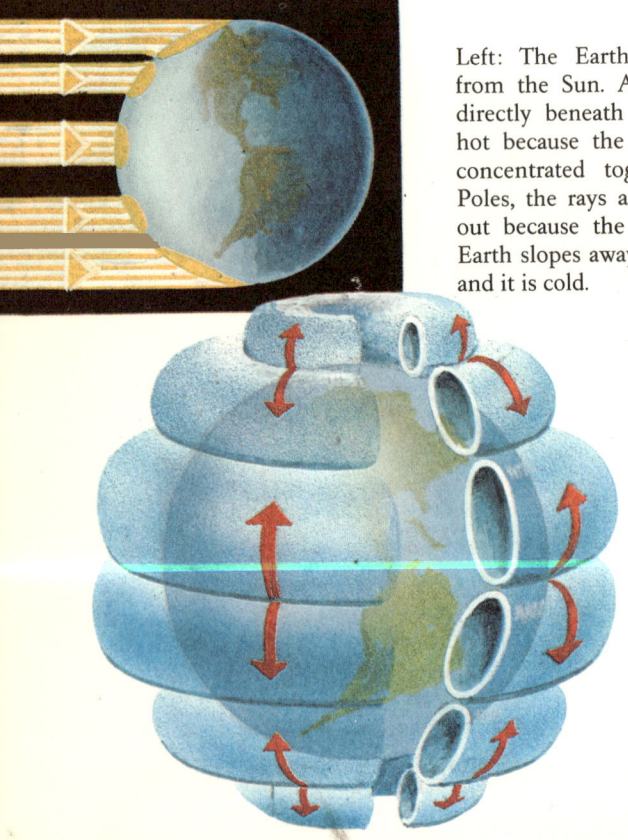

Above: At the Equator, the Sun's heat makes the air rise. It then flows away from the Equator before cooling and sinking. Two great air movements form, as shown by the red arrows. Differences in temperature also produce more air movements towards the Poles.

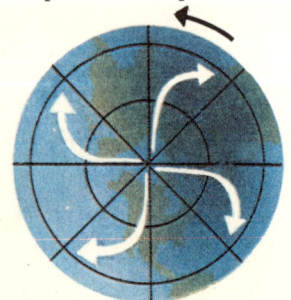

Left: As air rises and falls, it produces winds because air flows from a place where it is falling to a place where it is rising. Winds therefore basically blow north-south over the Earth. However, the rotation of the Earth causes them to veer to the right in the northern hemisphere and to the left in the southern hemisphere.

Above: A map of the world's winds. In the tropics the trade winds blow towards the Equator, blowing from the north-east in the northern hemisphere and from the south-east in the southern hemisphere. At the Equator it is often very calm because it is here that air is rising. The other main air movements nearer the Poles produce westerly winds in both northern and southern hemispheres. In the northern hemisphere, they blow over the oceans and bring rain to the western sides of continents.

Above: Although rain is always falling to the ground somewhere or other, the total amount of water in the world does not change. As some water falls from the air (thick arrows), so invisible water vapour is rising from plants and from bodies of water into the air (thin arrows). This water vapour eventually condenses to form rain. This movement of water is called the water cycle.

Does Life Exist on Other Planets?

Space scientists are fairly certain now that no life can exist on the Moon or on the other planets in our Solar System — these worlds are too cold or too hot, or they have no air or an atmosphere that will not support life. However, they have no way of telling whether life is likely to be found elsewhere in the Universe.

The Sun is only one of 100,000 million stars in our Galaxy, and scattered throughout the Universe there are millions of other galaxies each made up of millions of stars. It would be absurd to suggest that out of the millions upon millions of stars in the Universe, the Sun is the only one to possess a life-bearing planet.

But, although life may exist out in the deeps of space, are we ever going to be able to find it? Have we any way of contacting other beings in the Universe? Well, we have already sent out a message to the stars. The American space probes Pioneer 10 and Pioneer 11 flew past Jupiter in 1973 and 1974.

The first probe is now speeding on towards the edge of the Solar System. It will leave it in 1987 and then drift on outwards towards the stars. Pioneer 11 is doing the same, although it will fly past Saturn on the way. Perhaps these probes will one day be found by some other beings far distant from our corner of space. If so, the probes carry a message for them. It is simply a small plaque carrying a picture of a man and a woman and diagrams showing where in the Universe the probe began its journey.

One problem with contacting other forms of life is time. The nearest star is $4\frac{1}{4}$ light-years away, which means that a two-way radio conversation would take at least $8\frac{1}{2}$ years just for each person to say hello.

Some enthusiasts are trying to detect radio messages from space in an endeavour to find out whether other forms of life are trying to contact us. It is difficult to know what form a message would take, although we have thought of how images could be transmitted (see page 39).

Left: A strange Japanese figure wearing what looks like a space helmet.

Right: Strange markings on a stone from the Peruvian Andes.

Below: An odd being portrayed in a prehistoric cave drawing from Africa.

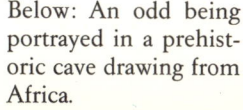

Left: An unusual drawing showing a princess being carried to a new world.

Moonbase

Our scene may portray a day on the Moon many years from now. The Earth rises in the black sky like a gigantic blue-white globe. It rises between a rocket ready to take off for Earth, and the gantry that supplies the rocket. The rocket does not look like today's rockets, for it is not going all the way to Earth, but only to an orbiting space station. As it will not enter the Earth's atmosphere, it does not need any casing and the fuel tanks show clearly.

In the foreground is an international Moonbase, mostly buried in the ground. A few domes rise from the surface, one containing an astronomical observatory. Beneath it are some workrooms, one containing green plants to replenish the oxygen in the air of the station just as green plants do on Earth. An operating theatre can be seen at the bottom of this section, and an eating room and dormitory in another section. Off this section leads an airlock. One person is donning a spacesuit and another has just left the airlock, perhaps to join his companions working on the surface. One is drilling into the surface to obtain samples of Moon rock while another stands by, ready to help if necessary. In the distance, a bulldozer throws some soil around a dome. The Moon does not have an atmosphere to protect its surface from meteors, and all the structures are buried as much as possible to prevent them from meteor damage. The members of the base are all working on scientific tasks connected with the Moon. The observatory is very important, because at times it is free from interference produced by the Earth and Sun.

Above: A design for an orbiting space station. In the future, spacecraft going to the Moon and planets may leave from a space station and return to it. Such spacecraft will not have to be built to withstand the strains of re-entering the Earth's atmosphere. Spacecraft like the space shuttle (below) will act as ferries between the station and the ground.

Below: The space shuttle is a new kind of space vehicle that is due to enter service in about 1980. It looks rather like an aircraft, although it

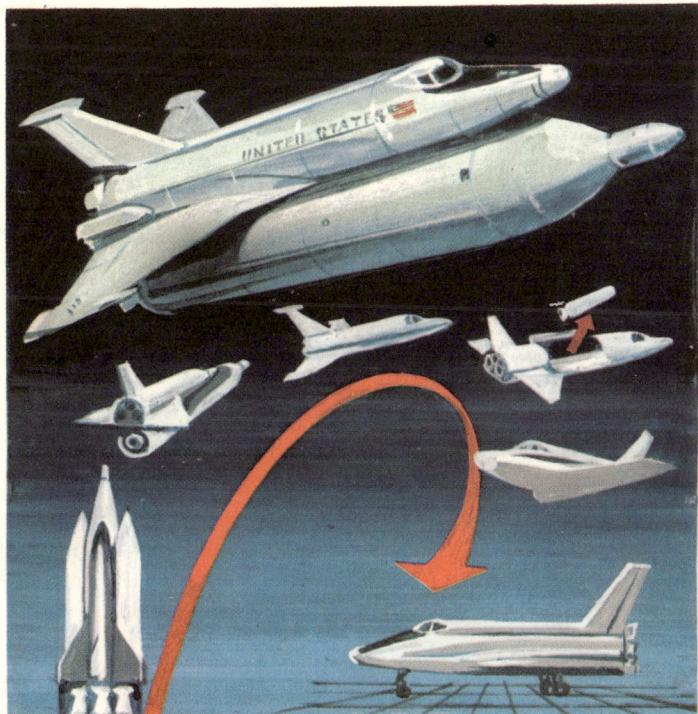

is rocket-powered. The shuttle leaves the ground fixed to a large booster rocket, which fires the shuttle on its way. It goes on into orbit and carries out its mission. It then returns to Earth and lands like an aircraft, so that it can be used again. Using a spacecraft several times will cut the cost of spaceflight considerably.

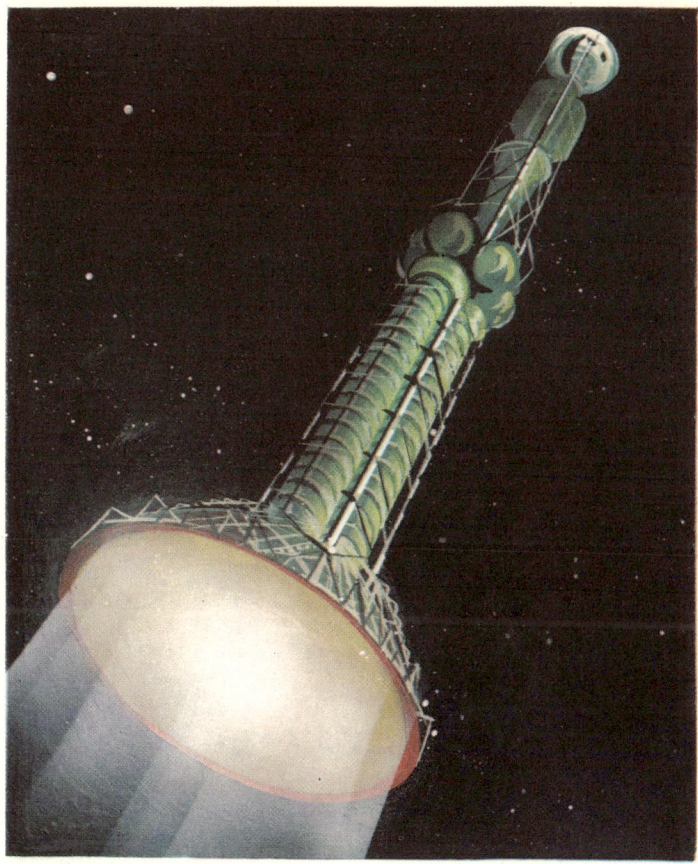

Above: Strange as it may seem, space rockets of the future may have bright beams of light shining from their bases. The light would act as a form of propulsion, because light does exert a very small pressure on objects. The light pressure of the Sun, for example, causes the tails of comets to stream out behind the head of the comet. The light rocket would not produce much power, but its light engine would work continually so that a great speed would slowly build up

Below: Astronauts might travel to the planets in spacecraft like these. The living quarters would be situated inside the ring, which would rotate so that artificial gravity would be produced inside and the spacemen need not be weightless for long periods.

INDEX

Air 58
Aldrin, Edwin 50, 54
Almagest 11
Andromeda Galaxy 21, 37
Apollo 18, 50, 51, 52, 54, 55
Aristarchus 10, 11, 24
Aristotle 10, 11
Armstrong, Neil 50, 54
Astrology 42
Astronaut 48, 49
Aurora 13

Black Hole 40
Brahe, Tycho 25, 27
Braun, Wernher von 45

Calendar 29
Comet 22, 23
Compass 32, 33
Constellation 30
Copernicus (crater) 19
Copernicus, Nicolas 24, 25, 26
Corona 13
Crater
    meteorite 23
    moon 19

Earth 14, 15, 16, 17
Eclipse 13, 19

Full Moon 19

Gagarin, Yuri 50
Galaxy 20, 21, 40, 41
Galileo 26, 34
Gemini (spacecraft) 51, 54
Glenn, John 50
Goddard, Robert 45

Gravity 18, 28, 46, 47
    artificial 61
Great Bear 30
Gyrocompass 33

Halley, Edmund 23
Hero of Alexandria 44
Herschel, Sir William 21
Hipparchus 11
Horoscope 42, 43

Jupiter 14, 15

Kepler, Johann 25, 27, 43

Latitude and Longitude 32, 33
Leonov, Alexei 50
Light, Speed of 12
Light Year 20, 21
Lippershey, Hans 34
Longitude See Latitude
Luna (space probe) 19
Lunar Module 55
Lunar Orbiter 19
Lunokhod 55

Mariner 15
Mars 14, 15
Mercury (planet) 14, 15
Mercury (spacecraft) 51, 54
Meteor 22
Meteorite 22, 23
Milky Way 20
Moon 18, 54, 55, 60
    eclipse 19
    full moon 19
    new moon 19
    phases 19